QUICK
LEATHER BINDINGS

Keith A. Smith

BOOK NUMBER 211

First Edition December 2002
First Edition, Second Printing April 2011

Published and distributed by keith smith *BOOKS*
1115 East Main Street
Suite 219, Box 8
Rochester, New York 14609-6152 USA
Fax: 585 482 2496
email orders: keith@keithsmithbooks.com
online: http://www.keithsmithbooks.com

Library of Congress Control Number: 2002 190293
ISBN: 0–9637682–9-8   ISBN 978-0-9637682-9-2

Non-Adhesive Binding Volume V

QUICK
LEATHER BINDINGS

Keith A. Smith

BOOK NUMBER 211

V

KE◉TH

keith smith BOOKS
Rochester, New York

for Alex & Jeanette Syndikas

QUICK Leather Bindings

PREFACE

One of my previous books, *Bookbinding for Book Artists,* brings traditional binding to the book artist without the expense of equipment or tools. Most of the bindings there used book cloth on the boards. Only one was presented in leather, rounded and backed—a very lengthy process.

My concern in this current book is not to show traditional binding, but to break away from it, yet to keep the structures strong and the materials archival. My aim is to strip away unnecessary steps and to find ways of speeding up those steps I cannot omit. The first thing is to eliminate any rounding and backing. This arched structure is used to support gigantic bindings of several hundred pages. Rounding and backing takes time and equipment. Even with makeshift equipment, it is a ponderous endeavor.

As a book artist, I don't need a binding of several hundred pages and, I suspect, neither does my reader. My needs are for bindings which can be constructed with up to a couple hundred pages. My desire also is to present elegant hard cover bindings in cloth or quarter leather, whichever is preferred. Some of the bindings I have devised for Volume V have only a single section. Other leather bindings described have two, three, four, or five sections—*quick* leather bindings! One to five sections containing from four to 100 pages meets the needs of most book artists.

LIMITED USE OF ADHESIVES: To speed things up, these structures are non-adhesive—the book blocks are attached by sewing. In my past books, for a totally non-adhesive binding a paper cover was sewn along with the text block.

Once hard covers were introduced, an adhesive was required. Even if the boards are sewn to the book block as with a Coptic sewing, decorative papers, applied with paste, cover the boards. This use of an adhesive is decorative, not part of the structure. If book cloth or leather is applied to the board it, too, requires an adhesive.

In Volume V, wheat paste, as well as glue, has been eliminated entirely. Not that I do not appreciate the qualities of paste, but my direction here is to speed up the process with a totally dry procedure. I hope you will find this direction in binding as enjoyable as I have. The methods shown in this book have been tested on my own books of my drawings, digital images and poetry over the past two years. Most of my own work now is large digital prints bound as single sheets, so I rely on the sewings in Volume IV, but I have eliminated any use of paste or glue. In speeding up my time spent binding, I thought I should pass along my ideas as Volume V.

TABLE *of* CONTENTS

INTRODUCTION

This is a book of new bindings which I have devised with hard cover, quarter cloth or leather and with no paste or glue—even for attaching leather.

For the book artist traditional leather binding is an enormous technical undertaking. The idea behind *Bookbinding for Book Artists* was to substitute all the equipment and tools to avoid the expense of setting up a bindery and to eliminate the need to pare leather. Still, the process is time consuming.

SPEED AND SIMPLICITY

This book you are reading presents a major simplification of the entire process of creating a leather binding. Here, I have done away with every step found in *Bookbinding for Book Artists* that could be eliminated. Those that could not be eliminated were simplified:

NO EQUIPMENT: In this book I throw out the press, the C–clamps, the hammer, dividers and weights. No sewing frame is needed.

FEW TOOLS: All tools are eliminated except needle and thread, scissors, bone folder, X-Acto™ knife and metal straightedge.

Furthermore, there will be no time spent rounding and backing—leave that to professional binders. There is no jaconette, no slitting or turning-in leather around notched boards. The cover boards have no notches.

QUARTER LEATHER, ONLY: By limiting the leather to the spine and extended onto the boards, there is not the frustration of messing with fussy leather corners at the foredge when making half, or full leather bindings. Unpared mitred leather turned in as corners on the inside of the board is almost always unsightly. Neat leather corners require thinly pared leather and there is no paring of leather in this book.

All new sewings are devised for Volume V. They are hard cover quarter cloth or leather containing no adhesives in the sewn structure. Leather and papers are adhered with 3M Positionable Mounting Adhesive™. No paste or glue is used in making these books.
This binding contains four sections, 64 pages. It is called *Hash Marks,* described on page 253.

One thing I have *added:* every binding described uses leather hinges for an elegant, as well as a durable hinge. Nothing looks nicer than to open the front cover and see the leather hinge extending from the endsheet onto the board.

leather hinge attached to the board

This sample binding of three sections is a hard cover, quarter leather binding with leather hinges. Color thread is inlaid between the hinge and the turn-ins at the head and tail.

Except for one binding which is cased-in, all bindings in Volume V are *continuous support sewings,* that is, the book block is sewn through the leather hinge and the leather spine. The leather hinge is not so much to hold in the book block, as to dress up the binding.

NO PASTE OR GLUE: Leather and decorative papers are attached to the board with Scotch Positionable Mounting Adhesive™. Sold by the roll, this is a dry, pressure-sensitive adhesive by 3M. See page 33.

Papers or leather backed with PMA go down instantly and you don't have to wait for anything to dry. There is no warpage from wet problems of paste—and the adhesive-backed leather and papers can be moved around until you are satisfied with their location before you fix them permanently to the board by burnishing. It's archival, too. As you can tell, I am very excited with this streamlining of the whole process of making various leather bindings *quickly.*

NO WAITING FOR LEATHER TO DRY: The leather is never pasted. There are no weights and no waits. Pasting leather is fine, but you have to wait hours for it to dry and keep the board under a weight so it will not warp. For this new approach to binding I threw out wheat paste altogether!

In the early stages of writing this volume I was going to attach the leather to the boards with PVA glue, which dries in under five minutes. When I worked out my first prototype with these streamlined procedures in March 2000, I was wary and a little sheepish. "What will bookbinders make of this?" I wondered. Later that month, Scott McCarney and I went to Australia to start seven weeks of teaching in various cities. First we went to Hobart. Penny Carey-Wells took us to the National Library of Tasmania. We met a wonderful conservator by the name of Stephanie McDonald. When I explained the concept of this new book on leather binding both Stephanie and Penny told us that (many) binders in Australia use PVA to attach their leather!

What a relief and vindication this was. Now I could write up this process for my next book without any misgivings. Gluing the leather with PVA would be quicker and that is the point of this book.

On the trip I was also introduced to kangaroo leather which can be purchased thinly shaved to 0.5mm. Later, I tried using the positionable mounting adhesive on the leather. To my great pleasure PMA goes on easily and the adhesive-backed leather clings to the board. I do *not* recommend it for heavier leather. I dismissed PVA glue—it can creep around and stain the front of the leather. Gluing is messy and I hate cleaning glue brushes; so do my students.

Volume V was coming into focus and becoming more of a departure from my past books on binding. Now that I've stated what I have discarded, it is time to show you results and describe how to make quick leather bindings.

Before I made these new sewings for Volume V, one of my favorite 1-section booklets was a pamphlet binding, not with a paper cover, but a hard cover book. The sewing does not show on the spine. The section is pamphlet sewn to a cloth or leather hinge which is cased-in.
In the past I have described this binding only as quarter cloth. With these new streamlined procedures I now can show this book as hard cover, quarter leather with leather hinges. It is fast and easy.

1-SECTION SEWINGS: The horizontal book and the one standing to the right are hard cover quarter leather bindings with leather hinges. To the left is a quarter cloth binding. Each contains a single section; 12 pages plus endsheets.

In each example the book block is sewn to the cover as a continuous support sewing. They are not cased-in, where the book block is attached only by the hinge. Sewing creates a stronger, more secure attachment, as are all but one book described in Volume V.

1-SECTION SEWINGS: On the left is a sewing titled *Exposed-Spine Board*. Three colors of leather are inlaid on the cover using positionable mounting adhesive. The book block is sewn to a wooden spine board which is only seen when the covers are opened.

The sewing in the middle and on the right is called *Faux Double Raised Cords*. The middle book is sewn with one color thread; the one on the right uses two colors.

There are four sewings described in Volume V which utilize a book block of a single section.

2-SECTION SEWINGS: These are three examples of 2-section continuous support sewings. New sewings were devised for Volume V with one-to-five sections for a range of choices. The binding on the right has inlaid quarter leather on the spine with no paring. It is described on page 179. There are six sewings described with two sections.

3-SECTION SEWING: This sewing was named *Darting Packed Stitch.* It is described on page 211. There are four sewings with three sections described.

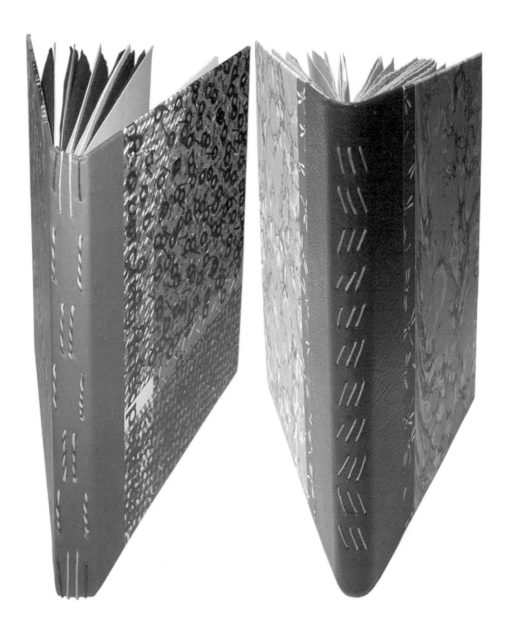

4-SECTION SEWINGS: Left is a 4-section continuous support sewing, titled *Spiralling Threads*. It is described on page 241. To the right is the other 4-section sewing described, page 253. It is called *Hash Marks*.

5-SECTION SEWING: This 80-page book is a continuous support sewing described on page 263. It is based on the Long Stitch through Slotted Wrapper Cover described in Volume I.

PRELIMINARIES

PARTS OF THE BOOK

OUTSIDE OF THE COVER

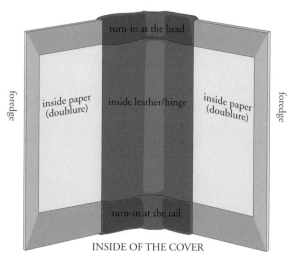

INSIDE OF THE COVER

The cover is completed before sewing. Book board is cut for each side cover. Quarter leather is applied to the boards, turned-in to the inside. The outside of the boards is covered with decorative paper, turned-in to the inside.

The leather hinge is fitted to the inside, unless casing-in. In that instance the leather hinge is sewn to the book block and then attached to the boards. See page 69.

The inside papers are attached finishing the cover. Only then is one of the continuous support sewings sewn through the leather spine.

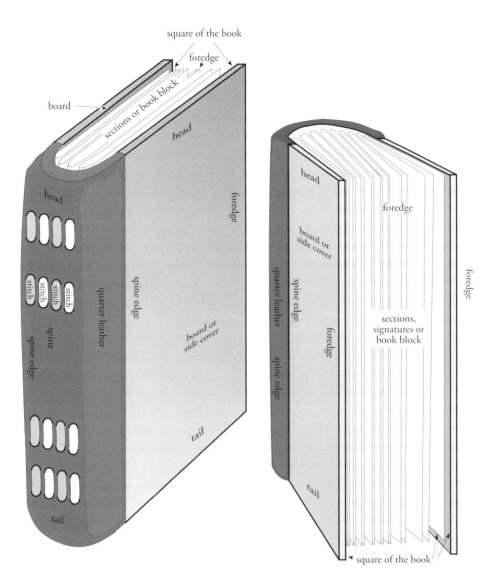

square of the book

foredge

board

sections or book block

head

head

foredge

head

spine edge

quarter leather

spine

spine edge

board or side cover

tail

stitch stitch stitch stitch

head

board or side cover

foredge

quarter leather

spine edge

foredge

spine edge

sections, signatures or book block

foredge

tail

tail

square of the book

There is no rounding or backing on these books and no spine board, although you can reinforce the spine with a strip of paper before adding the hinge.

CONTINUOUS SUPPORT: The example on the left shows a pattern of stitches with color thread/s used in the sewing decorating the spine. This creates a continuous support sewing. All but one of the books described in Volume V are continuous support sewings.

CASED-IN: If it were a cased-in binding, sewing would be on the hinge only. The adhesive on the hinge would be all that attaches the book block to the case.

MATERIALS
& TOOLS

Like the other volumes of *Non-Adhesive Binding,* there are few tools and no equipment needed for these bindings. In fact, there are fewer tools even though these are hard cover quarter leather bindings.

A couple items not in the other books must be added to this chapter. One is a list of sources for leather. Another is the adhesive I am encouraging you to try in these bindings, Scotch™ 568 Positionable Mounting Adhesive.

LEATHERS

SHAVED: It is critical in binding with unpared leather to use skins which have been shaved very thin. Bringing the quarter leather around the head and tail will cause a large bulge with thick leather. I suggest you purchase leather shaved to 0.5mm. Filler will be unnecessary when thin leather is used.

metal straightedge

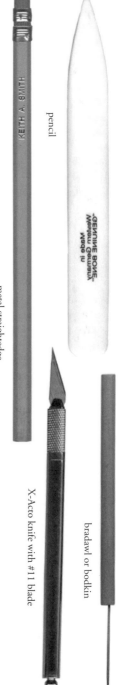

bone folder

pencil

X-Acto knife with #11 blade

bradawl or bodkin

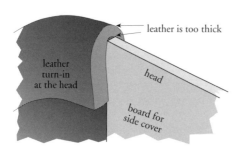

leather is too thick

leather turn-in at the head

head

board for side cover

FILLER: A scrap sheet of thick paper, referred to as *filler,* might be glued to the remainder of the board tangent to the quarter leather to bring the bare surface of the board up to the height of the leather. I do not use fillers. See page 93.

Kangaroo Hides

Perhaps it is my fondness for Australia, but I have been working mostly with kangaroo hides for the prototypes for Volume V.

Kangaroo is a lovely skin, moderately priced, and you can order online:

Packer Tanneries, Boundary Road
Narangra, Queensland
P O Box 113 Kallangur 4503 Australia
Carolyn_Hasemann@packertanning.com

COLORS: From Packer Tanneries, request samples of dyed kangaroo in 14 colors, as well as natural, vegetable tanned. Order undyed (Natural) or specify color.

FINISH: Hides come finished in lacquer coating or unfinished. I recommend unfinished.

THICKNESS: The skins come unshaved as well as in various thicknesses. Since you are not paring, you will want the leather as thin as possible. Specify "shaved to 0.5mm thickness."

If you wish an assortment of colors of small rectangles of kangaroo for the spine and hinges, packets can be ordered from:

Hollanders in Kerrytown
407 N. Fifth Avenue
Ann Arbor, MI 48104 USA
Tel: 734 741 7531
http://www.hollanders.com

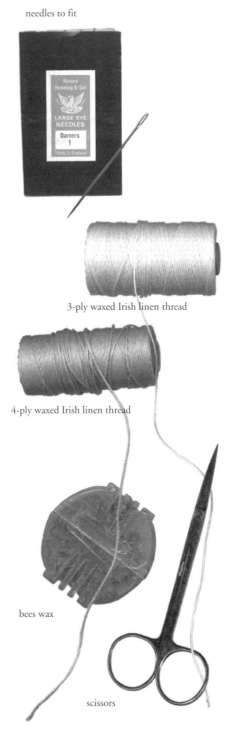

needles to fit

3-ply waxed Irish linen thread

4-ply waxed Irish linen thread

bees wax

scissors

Samples of kangaroo hides can be ordered online from Packer Tanneries:
<Carolyn_Hasemann@packertanning.com>

Calf and Goat Skins

Bookcraft Supplies
  Attn Mrs D M Tomlinson
  273 Longhurst Ln
  Mellor Cheshire England SK6
  5PW 061 427 7348
Bookmakers Intl.
  6701B Lafayette Avenue
  Riverdale MD 20737
  301 927 7787
Colophon Book Arts Supply Inc
  3611 Ryan Rd SE
  Lacey WA 98503-3860
  360 459 2940
  Fax 360 459 2945
Harcourt Bindery
  51 Melcher Street
  Boston, MA 02210
  617 542 5858
  Fax 617 451 9058

Harmatan Leather Ltd
  Westfield Ave,Higham Ferrers
  Northamptonshire
  NN9 8Ax England
  933 312471
  Fax 0933 412242
Moore & Pearsall Leathers Ltd 47
  Front St E Toronto ONT M5E
  1B3 Canada
  416 363 5881   30 colors.
  Color chart available.

Game Skins

Commanchero Traders
  Paul & Bonnie Range
  Rt2 Box 511
  Burnet TX 78611
  512 756 8844 Source for brain-
  tanned elk, vegetable-tanned
  deer and other cured game
  skins.

Book Cloth

Some people will prefer not to use the hides of animals. All the bindings in this book can be made in quarter cloth bindings. Any good binders' supply will sell book cloth. Some, of course, are better than others offering not only the commonly seen cloths, but also satins, taffetas and exotic surfaces. You can also make your own book cloth with the adhesive backing. See: *Make Your Own Book Cloth,* page 39.

THREAD

It is good to start collecting— especially papers and thread. I just ordered all 17 colors offered of 2-ply Irish linen thread and all 34 colors of 4-ply. A fine source: Royalwood, Ltd.

517 Woodville Road
Mansfield, Ohio 44907
1 800 526 1630
www.Royalwoodltd.com

For a small fee they will send a chart of all the colors and all diameters: 2-, 3-, 4-, 7- and 12-ply! They also have the best prices I have found.

It is important to have as many colors as you can afford so you can choose which to use on a particular binding.

PAPERS

Nothing is dearer to me in this process than papers—Japanese and Italian especially, but I have hundreds of decorative papers from many countries.

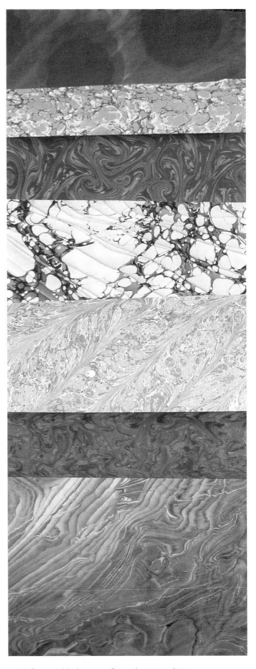

A few marbled papers from the United States

29

In the United States there many fine marblers and no certain one I patronize. I am always excited to find different papers when I meet a marbler.

Every city I visit usually has a store that I have frequented in the past and I make sure to stop in and buy more papers. There are too many good ones to list, so I will not.

My collection is not something to store, but to have on hand from which to make my selections with each new book. What finer luxury than flat files full of various papers waiting to be selected.

It is important to buy papers as you see them. Don't wait. In the early 1970s wanting to buy a particular sheet, Mrs. Aiko said the paper had been made by only two people in Japan—one had retired and the other moved to the city to make more money. The paper was extinct.

Last December I was back at Aiko's Art Materials Import in Chicago, and there were some beautiful papers on the counter. I asked Charles Izui if he had more of these. He said, "no," and that there would not be any more of these particular printed papers. I bought them knowing how precious they are. It is sad that many more decorative papers will probably stop being made as artisans grow old and the craft is not carried on by others.

Decorative papers from Japan and Italy

Keith Smith, *Miniature Version of Book Number 210,* August 2002. This edition of 5 copies of digital imagery has a continuous support sewing described on page 263. 18 x 14 x 2 cm.

As I often do, each copy is bound with varying colors of leather and different endsheets and marbled papers on the inside of the boards. Sometimes even the pictures and text may vary from book to book as I revise and alter between binding one copy to the next.

Even the dimensions can vary. Book 210 is also available in an edition of 20 in a single sheet Coptic sewing. The larger book is 44 x 35 x 3.5 cm.

A copy of Book 210 is reproduced in color on the cover of Volume V. That copy has 7 leathers inlaid on the spine. Of course, that is *my* copy of the edition.

568 POSITIONABLE MOUNTING ADHESIVE

All the bindings in this book are non-adhesive. However, since all have hard covers and wooden boards are not used, an adhesive is needed for the quarter covering and papers for the boards.

Scotch 568 Positionable Mounting Adhesive will be used to attach the quarter leather, book cloth and decorative papers to the boards. Of course, any of the bindings described can be approached more traditionally by adhering leather and paper to the boards with wheat paste. Instructions for making and using paste is in *Bookbinding for Book Artists* and Volume IV, *Smith's Sewing Single Sheets.* Instructions for PVA gluing are also found in Volume IV.

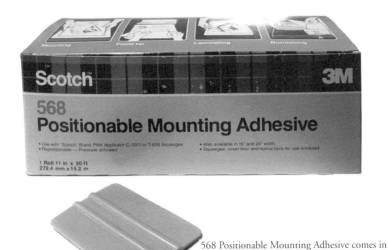

568 Positionable Mounting Adhesive comes in three widths, 11, 16 and 24 inches by 50 feet. On the left is the squeegee used for burnishing.

PROPERTIES OF THE ADHESIVE

ARCHIVAL CONCERNS: First off I must say never substitute some other backing adhesive, such as Witchstitch™. As far as I know, only Scotch™ 568 Positionable Mounting Adhesive claims to be archival.

THE ADHESIVE IN ROLLS: Scotch™ 568 Positionable Mounting Adhesive comes in rolls 11, 16 and 24″ wide by 50′ in length. With each roll comes a Scotch™ 568 Positionable Mounting Adhesive Liner and a squeegee.

LINER and SQUEEGEE: The liner is a stick-free surface laid on the table before unrolling the adhesive. It protects the surface of the table. The squeegee burnishes your leather, book cloth or paper to the adhesive. This is described under *Procedure,* page 36.

NOTE: In the remainder of this chapter, leather, book cloth or paper will be referred to as your *item.*

HOW IT STICKS: The roll is extended and the item is laid on the adhesive and tacked down. This is elaborated under *Procedure.* After trimming the item from the roll pressure is applied with the squeegee The adhesive consists of bubbles, pressure activated. The adhesive sticks permanently to your cloth or paper when busted by burnishing. The bubbles permit the adhesive sheet to be adjusted, thus "repositionable".

SAVE SCRAP BACKING PAPERS: The term *scrap backing sheet* will refer to the adhesive sheet after the adhesive has been peeled off so that all that remains is the slick paper resembling the liner paper.

Save each scrap backing sheet. All the adhesive lifts from it and it can be used as a liner; adhesive will not stick to the scrap backing sheets.

Scrap sheets are placed over leather before burnishing, pages 67 and 70. They are used in backing your own cloth, page 39. The are used in trimming leather turn-ins, page 72.

EFFICIENT USE OF THE ADHESIVE ROLL: For economical use of the adhesive I choose which width roll to use for a particular item and which direction to place it on the roll. I try never to leave bare areas on the adhesive.

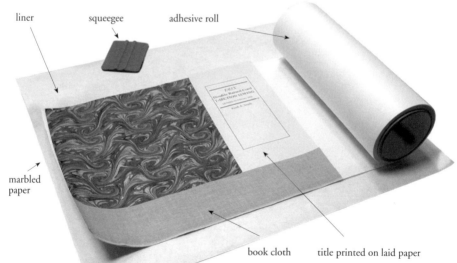

liner   squeegee   adhesive roll

marbled paper

book cloth   title printed on laid paper

Arrange items to be backed on the roll for the most efficient use of the adhesive. When there is an unused area of adhesive, back an extra piece of decorative paper for future use.

After placing the item which I need to back onto the adhesive, I fill any blank areas of adhesive with extra piece/s of decorative paper.

These papers will not only protect your straightedge from touching a patch of the adhesive, but uses all the surface of the expensive adhesive.

These extra pieces are backed, trimmed and saved for future use. This really aids my approach to covering boards, which relies on inlays of two or more decorative papers used in the design of the covers.

Advantages of the Positionable Mounting Adhesive

- Archival
- The roll doesn't dry out.
- Backed items can be kept for months before peeling off the backing and adhering them.
- Fast to apply and no waiting for the board to dry.
- No stretching of the papers.
- No warpage of the board from moisture of paste or glue.
- Inlaying papers is slightly more difficult because you are cutting through more plies of paper. It is not that much harder, and I find slippage is not the problem I thought it would be. Positioning the papers butted tightly one piece to next is possible, though not as fool-proof as with wheat paste. No warpage insures a perfect fit because there is no moisture as in pasting. See: *Inlaid Papers,* page 117.
- Commercial book cloth can be attached to the boards with this adhesive backing. Use a thin book cloth with less curl. Book cloth tends to curl because it probably has been stored tightly rolled. Cut the book cloth for quarter binding with the curl from head to tail, not from spine edge to foredge. This will avoid the curl factor from wanting to lift the vertical edge of the cloth once it is adhered to the board. A thinner book cloth is less apt to want to lift.
- Make your own book cloth. Backing your own fabrics is possible without a great deal of difficulty. See: *Making Your Own Book Cloth,* page 39.

Disadvantages

- Sticky. The adhesive must be handled carefully, as it is sticky. This is not a problem when handled properly.
- Expensive. The adhesive is relatively expensive, especially when compared to wheat paste.
- Slippery.
- Waste: Need to measure papers and leather slightly larger than needed, so that after the adhesive is applied and the backing paper is still in place, the item can be trimmed to the dimensions needed on a self-seal mat.

I find it is easier to cut with the good side of the item facing up. Line the item up with the grid on the cutting surface. be cautious because the backing paper is slippery and difficult to keep aligned to trim. Try trimming with the good side of the item face down and see which is easier for you.

Buy a 500 pack of #11 blades preferably a generic brand at a fraction of the cost.

- Cannot use scissors which get gummy and sometimes tear the paper. But this is no problem: Rather than using scissors, corners are cut with a #11 blade and X-Acto knife on a self-seal mat.
- No deckled edges. All items with backing must be trimmed with a straightedge and blade. Torn or deckled edge would permit small amounts of the adhesive on the top surface of your board. It becomes dirty because it is gummy and is next to impossible to clean off.

PROCEDURE APPLYING THE ADHESIVE

Using the roll of adhesive takes a little getting used to. Don't be discouraged. It is not difficult, even easy if you take proper precautions. Learn from my experience (mistakes). Once you become experienced using it, you will appreciate how quick it is to cover a board. Then you can use the boards immediately; there is no waiting for it to dry.

1. *SETTING UP:* To begin, always lay the liner on a smooth surface to keep any adhesive from getting on the table.

2. Cut the item *slightly larger* than than the finished dimensions needed. After the backing is applied the item will be trimmed to the precise final dimensions in step 9.

3. Roll out the adhesive, sticky side up for a length slightly longer than the paper or cloth you will be using.

4. Place the item with the unfinished side against the adhesive. Line up the item with the horizontal edge of the adhesive closest to you. Drape the item across the adhesive. Reposition item if necessary, but try to avoid this by carefully lining up as you lay the item down the first time.

5. Press lightly with the palm of your hand from the center out to the edges to release any large air bubbles before using the squeegee. This will tack down the item lightly.

If the paper or book cloth is warped, you may have to burnish lightly with the squeegee to insure the item is tacked down before trimming. Use the 3M squeegee which comes with the adhesive roll to stroke lightly from the center of the item outward to make sure it temporarily tacked down.

NOTE: Never burnish directly on leather or dark color laid paper. You will make it shiny. Lay the item face down and burnish with the squeegee on the backing paper before it is peeled off. If the item is already attached to the board, lay a scrap of the backing paper on top before burnishing.

6. *TRIMMING THE ITEM FROM THE ROLL:* Carry the roll with the item temporarily tacked in position to a self-seal cutting mat. Lay the straightedge on the item adjacent to the bare adhesive.

    Protecting the straightedge: If the item does not completely cover the width of the adhesive, even if it is just a thin sliver of exposed adhesive, place a scrap backing paper beside the item over the exposed area prior to placing your straightedge on the item. Otherwise your straightedge will stick to the adhesive and become gummy.

    With one cut, trim the item from the roll. Place the roll back on the table away from the self-seal mat.

NOTE: Always place the straightedge on the item, not on the bare adhesive. Place the straightedge very slightly in on the item rather than trying to cut precisely on the edge of the item and the bare adhesive. This will give you a clean cut which will serve as the final cut for that edge of the item.

    Also, if you were to cut exactly on the edge between the adhesive and the item, you might leave a small edge of adhesive beyond the item. When you apply the item to the board this risks an edge of adhesive on the cover which will give a gummy edge on your cover.

7. Trim any exposed adhesive from the item by cutting slightly in on the item. This is not the final trimming, but removes any adhesive extending from the edge of the item.

8. *FINAL BURNISHING:* Take the item to the table and place on the liner face down. Make sure the liner is free from tiny scarps or any gummy areas from the adhesive.

    Burnish with the squeegee stroking from the center to the outside. Turn the item 90° and burnish again. Turn the paper again and burnish.

Final Trimming Procedure

9. Trimming is done after the adhesive is applied to the paper or cloth and *prior* to peeling off the backing. Cut on a clean self-seal cutting mat.

    Trimming can even be done after the backing is removed: Lay a scrap piece of backing on your self-seal cutting surface. Place the paper with the *adhesive side towards the scrap backing.*

This will prevent your straightedge from being covered with adhesive and will prevent the adhesive from lifting from the paper or cloth where you laid the straightedge directly on the adhesive.

BLADE: Use a #11 X-Acto blade or a blade equally as thin. You must use *a new blade.* A dull blade will not give a clean cut and can rip the paper.

CUTTING: Trimming your good paper with the adhesive and backing paper attached dulls blades rapidly. A dull blade will tear rather than cut your marbled/laid paper. You must change to a new blade often.

Peeling the Item from the Adhesive Backing

10. Start the separation between backing sheet and item with your thumbnail.
   SMALL STRIP OF PAPER: If the item is a thin strip, the backing peels off with no resistance.

   LARGE AREA ITEM: Start the separation and lay the large item face up. The broader the area of the item the more pressure is needed in peeling. If you were to hold the item with one hand and place your thumb on the adhesive surface while you peeled off the item, your thumb would stick. Instead, after you have started peeling at a corner, slip a scrap backing sheet onto the adhesive. Then you can press down with only as much pressure as needed to peel the large item from the adhesive backing. All the adhesive will lift from the backing sheet.

   IF ONLY PARTIALLY ADHERED: If you have not burnished thoroughly, when you start to peel off the backing, part of the adhesive will bubble and stretch, clinging to the backing sheet. This can be corrected. Lay the the item face down on the liner . Burnish with the squeegee only in the problem area. Resume peeling off the backing paper.

Applying Adhesive-Backed Leather to the Boards

To apply the quarter cloth or quarter leather which has been backed with the adhesive to the board, see: *Applying Leather to the Boards,* page 67.

Applying Adhesive-Backed Paper to the Boards

To apply a single sheet of decorative paper to cover the remainder of the outside of a board for a quarter leather binding, first see: *Filler,* page 93, then see: *Paper for the Outside of the Boards,* page 95.

To apply several pieces of decorative paper to cover the remainder of the outside of a board for a quarter leather binding, first see: *Filler,* then see: *Inlaid Papers,* page 117.

MAKING YOUR OWN BOOK CLOTH

You can back fabrics—your own choice of piece goods (yard goods). Limit your choice of fabric to something fairly thin and not too bulky.

If you have ever tried to add a paper backing to cloth or to coat cloth with paste or PVA glue you know how extremely difficult that process is. Not so much here. It is a great deal easier with the backing adhesive.

1. Iron the fabric. Don't attempt an extra long piece of cloth. Use just enough for a single cover. Height of the fabric is the same or less than the width of the roll.

2. Extend the roll of adhesive. Cut it slightly longer than needed. Cover all but the left vertical edge of the sheet of adhesive with scrap PMA backing. Lay the cloth in position on the scrap backing, but not on the exposed adhesive.

3. Lift the left vertical edge of the fabric into position on the exposed strip of adhesive. Pull the scrap backing which is between the fabric and the adhesive to the right to remove it.

4. Lightly run the palm of your hand across the fabric from the center out to the edges to release any large air bubbles. Do this again with only slightly more pressure so the fabric seems flat with no air bubbles.

5. Turn the fabric over onto a larger scrap of backing paper. With the fabric towards the table, the backing with the adhesive will be facing up.

6. Use the 3M squeegee to adhere the adhesive to the cloth. Turn the fabric face up. Cover it with a scrap piece of the adhesive backing paper. Burnish. Never burnish directly on the cloth. This will help prevent stretching the fabric when you burnish the cloth to the adhesive.

    Firmly stroke with the squeegee on top of the backing sheet from the center to the edges. Turn the fabric/adhesive 90° and again use the squeegee from the center to the edges. This will insure the fabric adheres to the adhesive backing. Put the removed backing sheet aside.

7. Place a scrap piece of the adhesive backing paper on your self-seal cutting mat. Trim the cloth with a rotary knife. An X-Acto knife will pull rather than cut. Trimming face down will help insure you will not snag the cloth.

8. Place a small amount of PVA glue on a brush. Run the brush across the edge of the cut fabric which will not be turned-in. Do not get glue on the surface of the cloth. This will seal and help prevent the cloth from fraying.

9. Place the cloth on the table with the backing on the liner or a scrap piece of backing paper with the fabric face down. See: *Peeling the Item from the Adhesive Backing* described on the previous page.

NOTE: As I peel the backing from the cloth, I keep inserting a scrap backing paper over the area of the exposed adhesive on cloth. Continue until you remove the backing and have the scrap paper lightly over the entire cloth.

COVERS

INTRODUCTION TO COVERS

The *cover* is the combination of the two boards, referred to as the *front* and *back covers* or *side covers* attached to each other across the spine with cloth or leather. The flat back binding has a third board in the center for the spine. This board is called the *spine board*. Since quarter cloth or leather does not cover the entire surface of the out-side of the side covers, the remain-der of the boards is covered with decorative paper before the cover is attached to the book block.

Casing-In

There is only one description of a cased-in binding in Volume V, page 111. The book block will be sewn to a cloth or leather hinge. See *pamphlet sewing*, beginning on page 158.

The book block and hinge are attached to the inside of the boards, referred to as *casing-in*.

All the other bindings in Volume V are described not as cased-in but sewn to the cover. This is referred to as *continuous support sewing*.

Continuous Support Sewings

In this approach the book block is not attached to the cover after sewing. The section/s are sewn through the spine of the cover. The cover becomes the sup-port. Unlike cord or tape supports, the entire spine is the support, thus continuous.

This is an ideal construction, a far better structure to the cased-in codex, since the book block will never fall out of the covers.

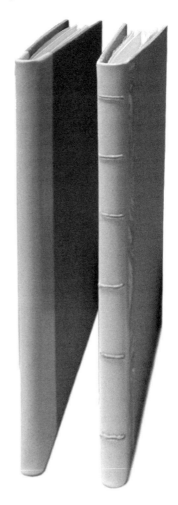

On the left is a sample of a *cased-in* codex containing one section. The quarter leather binding on the right has one sec-tion as a *continuous support sewing*.

QUARTER LEATHER

QUARTER LEATHER ONLY: In making a cover the two boards are attached to each other. The leather may not cover the entire board, which is a *full leather binding.* If it only extends part way onto the boards at the spine edge, this is referred to as *quarter leather.*

If a quarter binding also uses leather to protect the corners of the board at the foredge, this combination is called a *half leather binding.*

NOTE: I will refer to *quarter cloth or leather* as simply *quarter leather* for brevity, but you can make any of the bindings in Volume V with either book cloth or leather, whichever you prefer.

1. Quarter leather binding   2. Half leather binding   3. Half leather binding

DON'T CUT CORNERS: Making leather corners is difficult enough using thinly pared leather. To upholster corners with unpared leather is a nightmare. It is described in *Bookbinding for Book Artists.* Volume V will not permit showing half or full leather bindings here, only quarter leather—it's *quick.* I've made my case. Now to show you how to make yours.

PROPORTION TO THE BOARD

aes•thet•ic n. "A guiding principle in matters of artistic beauty and taste; artistic sensibility: 'a generous Age of Aquarius aesthetic that said that everything was art' (William Wilson)." –American Heritage Dictionary

Quarter leather literally means a fourth of the board is covered with leather. Poetic license permits aesthetic judgement. Use your eyes, not your ruler.

Below, left, are three various widths of "quarter" leather applied to bare boards. To the right, each is shown as a finished book to demonstrate the proportion of leather to the remainder of the board:

1. In this example there is not enough leather to attach to the boards securely. See illustration on page 46. To suggest narrow leather, use wider leather then overlap the leather with paper to suggest narrow leather, page 47.

2. Usually a narrow to medium strip of leather can be elegant. Amount of leather is determined by the paper color and design.

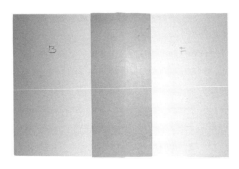 

3. Here, the leather covers a quarter of the board, which is a mathematical, not a visual decision. It is too bulky.

bare board exposed where leather lifted

The quarter leather was not wide enough to securely attach to the side covers. It adhered for a week, but after opening and closing, the leather popped off the front board. Now it is attached only at the head and tail, rather than all along the marbled strip pf paper.

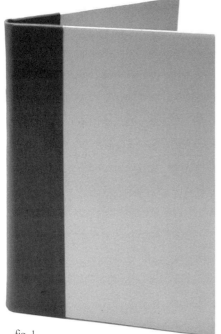

fig. 1

fig. 2

fig. 3

Procedure to avoid the pop-up of a narrow strip of leather as on the facing page:

1. Adhere a wider strip of leather than you wish to show. This will securely attach the leather to the boards. The leather must cover the hinge.

2. Add filler to the remainder of the board to the exact height of the leather. Apply the decorative paper which will appear tangent to a narrower strip of leather. Actually, it will sit on top of the leather.

3. Finish covering the board with decorative paper. The finished cover appears to have a narrow strip of leather on the board.

CASED-IN: Casing-In is described on page 111. Above is the outside view of the case. Front of the boards are finished with quarter leather and paper on the remainder of the boards.

Below is the inside view of the case with the optional inlaid threads which will be in the seam between the turn-ins and the hinge. Inside papers are added after the hinge and book block are adhered. Gap between the boards was made for a 1-section book block.

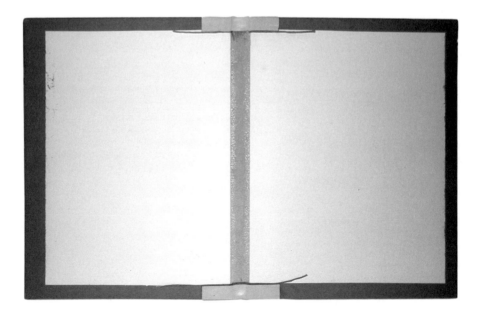

CASED-IN: Above, the leather hinge has been backed with adhesive. Sewing stations have been pierced in the section and correspondingly on the hinge, ready to be sewn.
Below, the hinge and section were sewn with a 5-hole pamphlet sewing ready to be cased-in.

CASED-IN: Above, the leather hinge has been attached to the boards or cased-in. Height of the hinge fits snugly to the optional inlaid threads. Width of the hinge and threads was made wider than necessary, to be trimmed after it is attached.

Below, Threads and hinge have been trimmed to the exact width of the turn-ins. The excess hinge was peeled from the board.

CASED-IN: The final step in finishing a cased-in binding is to adhere the paper to the inside of the boards.

The sample binding shown on pages 48–51 has inlaid thread between the seam of the inside leather or hinge and the turn-ins at the head and tail. I prefer to finish the seam with a thin strip of inlaid leather rather than inlaid thread. See example on the following page. Instructions for inlaying strips of leather are on page 88.

CONTINUOUS SUPPORT SEWING: Continuous support sewings begin on page 129.
Above is the outside view of the cover.

Below, the inside of the cover is completely finished prior to any continuous support sewing. The leather hinge, or *inside leather,* is applied between the turn-ins prior to sewing a continuous support sewing.

Below, the sewing stations have been pierced in the book block and the corresponding stations on the spine.

PRE-PLANNED POSITION OF THE LEATHER INLAYS WITH THE SEWING STATIONS: Position of the sewing stations should be designed to fit the inlays of leather on the outside and inside of the cover. Stations should not be in the seam between pieces of leather or very close to the seam. Taking the needle through could lift the leather. Stations can extend onto large turn-ins at the head and tail, as shown on the facing page.

Placement of the leather on the spine was planned *before* the leather was inlaid on the spine. No sewing station arbitrarily falls in or near a seam, as shown on the left.

Likewise, the leather inlays on the inside of the cover take into consideration where the stations will be pierced, as shown in the illustration at the bottom of the facing page.

Another design element is seen in the photo at the bottom of the facing page: For a different look, the turn-ins have been exaggerated. Large strips of leather are inlaid between the turn-in and the center leather of the hinge. Paper for the inside of the boards becomes dwarfed.

NOTE: The pierced stations in the cover are paired at the head and tail, with a single vertical row in the middle. This gives the look of a multi-section sewing, but the book block is a single section. The head and the tail are a sewing called *Faux Double Raised Cords,* page 141. The center of the spine is Sewn Chains, described in Volume II, Non-Adhesive Binding, *1- 2- & 3- Section Sewings.*

CONTINUOUS SUPPORT SEWING: Inlaid leather on the outside of the boards is described on page 181. Instead of inlaid threads on the inside of the boards, strips of leather were inlaid as shown on the facing page and described on page 88.

Keith Smith, Book Number 213, August 2002. Digital imagery. Edition of 5. 19 x 14.5 x 1.5 cm.

CONTINUOUS SUPPORT SEWING: Each copy of an edition of my books is finished differently. Inside view of the cover of this copy of Book 213 shows different treatment of the boards and different colors of leather. The same sewing is used as that on the previous page. As in some single section sewings in Volume V, the sewing extends from beneath the section, across the spine to the board. In the above example, the two stations at the head and tail extend, but the middle sections are a single row of stations beneath the fold of the single section book block. This horizontal lines of exposed stitches at the head and tail are a design element. See sewings on pages 135, 141, 149 and 157.

Indirectly related to this design is the treatment of the paper. After the PMA was added to the marbled paper, but before the backing was peeled, a vertical line of holes was punched. When the paper is applied to the board the paper beneath is seen through the holes.

TRADITIONAL 3-BOARD COVERS

The traditional 3-board cover is used only for casing-in a multi-section flat back.

Since the only book block cased-in described in Volume V has a single section, there is no need to describe a cover with a spine board. For information on 3-board covers see *Bookbinding for Book Artists*.

Design ideas often come from elements in traditional binding, such as the spine board. Some binders have flaunted it by exposing the spine board on the outside of the cover. In such instances it is generally made of metal or wood to add another texture. See pages 57–59.

In that vein, one sewing for Volume V has an exposed-spine board, but it is only seen on the inside of the cover. See page 157.

A 3-board cover is used in casing-in a multi-section flat back. The 3-board cover is not used for any sewing in Volume V.

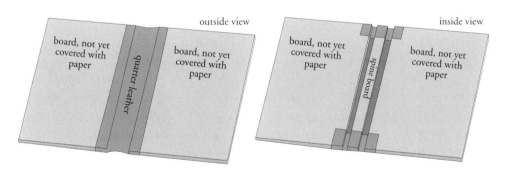

TRADITIONAL 3-BOARD COVER: No spine board will be described in Volume V. It is difficult to press the leather against the depth of the boards without distorting the right angle of the turn-ins and there are 8 depths of boards on a 3-board cover. This complicates lining up the inside leather/hinge with the turn-ins. Instead, a spine paper will be used to reinforce the stiffness of the spine.

EXPOSED-SPINE BOARDS

Introduction

Generally a 3-board cover is used only on a multi-section sewing, cased-in. It is difficult to cut a thin spine board for a 1- or 2-section sewing, as well as of no purpose.

An exception was made designing the *Exposed-Spine Board*, page 157. It is not cased-in but uses a thin spine board the same thickness as the covers. Also, see page 151.

In Volume V continuous support sewings do not use a spine board, but use spine-paper. See page 76. Paper stiffens and gives shape to the leather on the spine. Sewings benefit from added reinforcement with spine paper.

Two Traditional Approaches to the Spine Board

The traditional approach for a 3-board cover is to have the leather turn-in over, and hiding, all three boards. A second, though less common traditional 3-board cover exposes a wooden spine board on the outside of the spine. These are dramatic objects which invite the viewer to pick them up and hold them. Examples are shown in Volume I as well as in the reproduction to the right by Michele Powers, also illustrated in Volume III.

Michele Powers, Long Stitch/Link Stitch, 1995.
14.5 x 13 x 1.5 cm.

This is an example of a wooden spine board placed on the outside of the cover prior to sewing. Side covers here are paper.

Exposed-Spine Board on the Inside of the Cover

In a variation of *Loop-Packed Tapes* the spine board is separate from the cover. Instead of placing it on the outside of the spine I have moved it to the inside of the cover. The spine shows only leather.

The book block is sewn to the spine board. Hardwood or a strip of copper or other metal is used. The second sewing attaches the spine board, and thus the book block, to the cover. Why? It permits the spine board to be exposed. This adds another texture seen only upon opening the book. If you like this approach, you can modify many sewings to be sewn to the spine board, then attach the exposed-spine board to the inside of the cover.

Spine boards often have been exposed, but on the *outside* of the cover, as in the example on the previous page.

The only thing different here is the wooden or metal spine board is hidden until the book is opened. It is non-conspicuous consumption, like having a mink coat, but only as a liner on a cloth coat. You get to feel the mink, but you are not showing it off to passers-by. At least that idea inspired my spine boards which are revealed upon opening the book, as shown on the next page.

DIMENSIONS OF EXPOSED-SPINE BOARDS: If the spine board is on the outside of the cover, it is the full width and height of the covers, as in the book by Michele Powers on page 57. Adhesive might be used to attach the wooden spine board to the cover. Usually, it is attached only by the sewing.

If the exposed-spine board is on the inside of the cover, the width and height is the same as the book block. Depth of the spine board is not critical. However, to keep the book block from extending beyond the foredge of the covers be sure to add the depth of the spine board to the width of the book block to determine how wide to make the side covers.

The gap between the boards is the width of the spine board plus a gap (hinge) on each side to permit the boards to close.

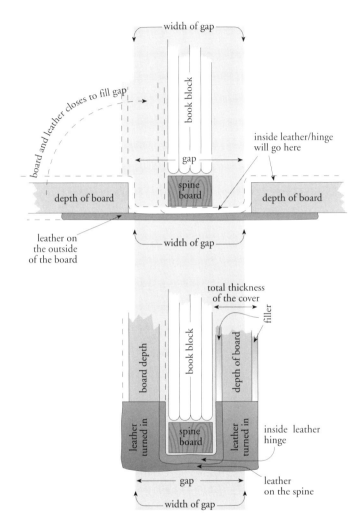

AN EXPOSED-SPINE BOARD INSIDE THE COVER:

The gap is determined in the same manner as with the 2-board cover.

Width of the spine board is the width of the book block.

Depth of the spine board is only relevant in that it will extend the width of the book block. Measure the width of the side covers, keeping in mind the width of the book block plus the thickness of the spine board.

The spine board is removed and the turn-ins are made. The inside leather is added the same as with a 2-board cover. See page 69 and page 158. Outside view of this cover looks similar to the traditional 3-board cover. This sewing, *Exposed-Spine Board,* is described on page 157.

NOTE: Width of the covers must accommodate the added thickness of the spine board: Width of the side covers is the width of the book block, *plus the depth of the spine board* and the square of the book.

2-BOARD COVERS

INTRODUCTION TO 2-BOARD COVERS

The 2-board cover will be used for all sewings in Volume V. It consists of the two side covers connected by quarter cloth or leather. The boards are cut and the outside leather is applied connecting the boards before you sew.

2-PLY SPINE: In casing-in, the book block is sewn to the inside leather/hinge. Then the leather hinge is applied to the inside of the boards tangent to the turn-ins at the head and tail. If optional inlaid threads are used, page 86, or inlaid strips of leather, page 88, the hinge extends to these items, rather than to the turn-ins. The outside leather and the hinge create a 2-ply leather spine.

In continuous support sewing, the leather hinge/inside leather is applied to the cover prior to sewing through this 2-ply leather spine.

3-PLY SPINE: A 2-ply leather spine is adequate to support sewing the book block to the cover in a continuous support sewing. However, I always reinforce the spine. The third ply is not a spine board, since you cannot sew through a board, but is made of paper or DuPont Tyvek™. This will be referred to as the *spine paper.* It is described on page 76.

Quarter leather long stitch sewing not described in this book. Cover is a self-portrait by Aatis Lillstrom, October 2002.

BOARDS FOR SIDE COVERS: For books under 9 x 12" I suggest you use mat board, as it is thinner than most book boards. The final side cover will be slightly thicker than the mat board if you build up the board to the height of the leather by adding a filler paper on both sides of the board. I rarely use fillers because my leather is very thin and the decorative paper almost as thick. Buy leather shaved to 0.5mm. thickness. If filler is desired to bring the paper up to the height of the leather, the completed book will have 3-ply side covers, the board plus filler on each side, shown on pages 79–83 and 93.

NOTE: If you do not know about grain, how to fold paper, how to make sections, sewing stations and how to tie knots, please refer to Volume I, *Books without Paste or Glue;* Volume IV, *Smith's Sewing Single Sheets,* or, to *Bookbinding for Book Artists.* It is not my intention to force you to buy another of my books in order to do the sewings in this one. I just hate to duplicate information that I have already stated in three other books.

Book Block

Fold down or compile your section/s for the book block. The dimensions of the boards are obtained from the section/s.

Measure and cut the boards slighter larger than the book block with an overhang at the head, tail and foredge. This is referred to as the *square of the book.* The square is generally 1 1/2 times the thickness of the board. (The board being mat board plus any fillers.)

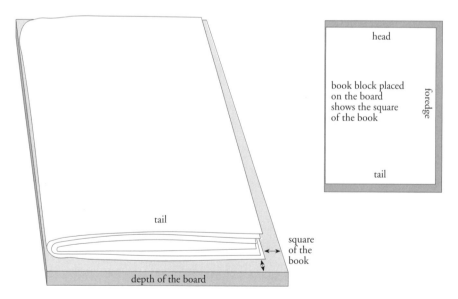

Square of the book, or *square,* is the amount of overhang of the boards to protect the book block. The square is usually 1 1/2 times the thickness of the board.

ABOVE: The spine has five pieces of leather inlaid. Brocade borders this. In the center of the boards is another strip of leather. The foredge of the board is covered with book cloth.

BELOW: Eleven pieces of leather are inlaid on the front of the boards, starting with the three turn-ins at the head. Next, the large horizontal strip is butted up, then the borders above and below it. Finally the turn-ins at the tail are added, then the papers, one at each foredge for easy upholstering of the corners. In this and the example above, no leather upholsters the corners—stretching the definition of quarter leather.

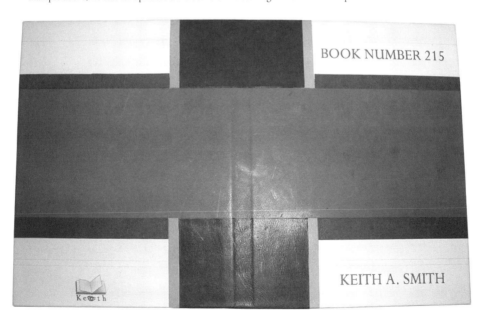

DETERMINING THE GAP BETWEEN THE BOARDS

1. Measure the depth of the unsewn book block slightly compressed. Add to this the thickness of 2 1/2 to 3 book boards plus two thicknesses of the leather for the total width of the spine, which is also the measurement of the *gap* between the two boards.
   Thickness of the leather is *critical.* See page 79.

2. Place the two side covers on the table. You will be looking at the inside of the side covers. Lay a straightedge under and tangent to the tail of the two boards to align them. Spread the boards apart to form the gap between the boards as measured in the previous step. Place strips of masking tape across the boards to temporarily fix, that is, stabilize the gap. Do not place tape within an inch of the head or tail; it will obstruct the turn-in of the leather.

3. Place the Positioning Adhesive Mounting Liner on the table. Flip the boards over onto the liner careful not to stretch the tape and alter the width of the gap determined in step 1. Stretching might also make the boards unparallel. You are now looking at the outside of the side covers.

4. Determine how far you want the leather to extend onto the boards. Measure in from the spine edge and mark a vertical pencil line lightly on the right board. This is the front cover. Symmetrically mark the other board, measuring in from the edge at the gap.

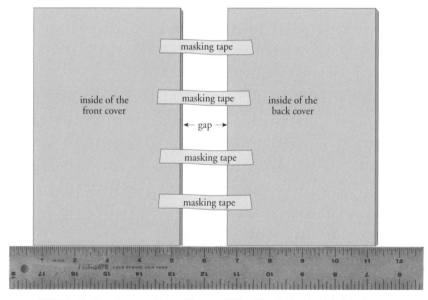

STEP 2: Fix the spine-gap with masking tape. This will be the inside of the boards.

MEASURING FOR QUARTER LEATHER

Width of the quarter leather is the distance from the pencil line on the left
  board, across the gap to the line on the right board.

Height of the leather is the height of the boards plus the *overhang* at the head
  and the tail which will be turned-in to the inside of the board. See: *fig. 1*
  on pages 74, 75 and *step 1,* page 76.

The overhang must be enough so the turn-ins will remain securely
attached. If the turn-in is less than 3/8″, opening and closing the board will
cause the leather turn-in to pop from the board.

Using 2-ply mat board, an overhang of 1/2″ will dwindle to a turn-in of
only 3/8″ because the overhang must go around the depth of the board.

The *minimum turn-in* must be 3/8″ at the head and 3/8″ at the tail. Total of
both turn-ins is 3/4″, requiring 1/2″ overhangs at each end. The height of
the leather for a minimum turn-in is the height of the boards plus 1″.

DO NOT CUT the leather to the finished dimensions. The leather will be
cut slightly larger in length and width, then trimmed to the finished
dimensions after the Positionable Mounting Adhesive has been placed on
the back of the leather.

Cut the leather slightly larger than the finished dimensions. Apply the
Positionable Mounting Adhesive as described on pages 33–39.

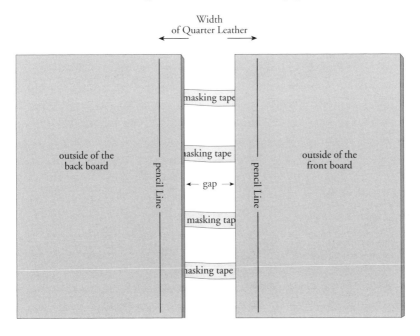

STEP 4: Mark the width of the quarter leather on the outside of the boards in pencil.

Use Leather Shaved to 0.5 mm Thickness

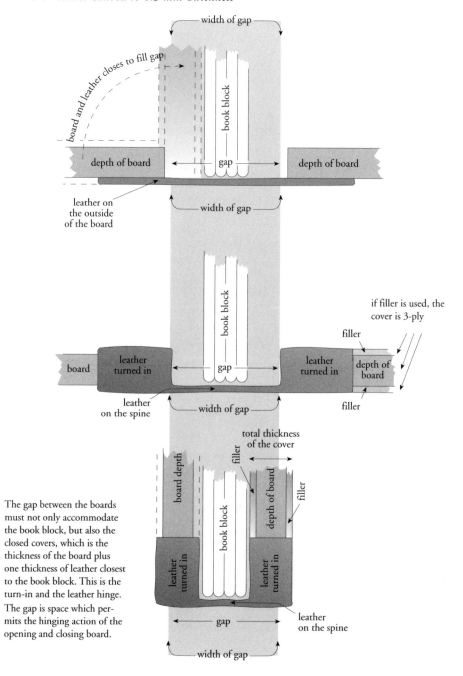

width of gap

board and leather closes to fill gap

book block

depth of board · gap · depth of board

leather on
the outside
of the board

width of gap

book block

if filler is used, the
cover is 3-ply

filler

board · leather
turned in · gap · leather
turned in · depth of
board

leather
on the spine · width of gap · filler

total thickness
of the cover

board depth · filler · depth of board · filler

book block

leather
turned in · book block · leather
turned in

gap

leather
on the spine

width of gap

The gap between the boards
must not only accommodate
the book block, but also the
closed covers, which is the
thickness of the board plus
one thickness of leather closest
to the book block. This is the
turn-in and the leather hinge.
The gap is space which permits the hinging action of the
opening and closing board.

APPLYING THE ADHESIVE TO THE LEATHER

Follow steps 1–10, *Procedure Applying the Adhesive,* beginning on page 36. Then follow the steps below titled *Applying Adhesive-Backed Leather to the Boards.*

APPLYING ADHESIVE-BACKED LEATHER TO THE BOARDS

After applying the adhesive to the quarter leather for the outside of the boards, making the final trim and peeling the backing from the leather, you are now ready to attach the leather to the boards.

The two boards for the side covers are taped together with the tape towards the table. The boards are laying on the liner. See drawing on page 65.

1. Hold the leather with a very light touch to keep the adhesive from sticking to your fingers. Align the leather slightly above the boards, centering the overhang at the head and tail. Lower the leather in place using one of the pencil lines as a guide. If it does not align properly with your pencil lines you can pick it up and reposition it. When you are satisfied, lightly press the leather with the palm of your hand, but only to the head and tail. Do not press on the overhangs. The overhangs of leather, merely resting on the liner, will not stick to it.

2. Flip the boards over. Turn-in the overhang at the head. Press firmly as you bring the leather around the depth of the board so the leather adheres to the edge of the board. Do not pull the leather onto the inside surface of the board; simply press downward. If you pull the leather onto the board it will stretch out of shape. You want to keep the leather turn-ins with edges that are right angles.
    Form the turn-in at the tail in the same manner.

3. Hold the boards in place while you remove the strips of masking tape.

4. Run a bone folder from the head, down the turn-in on the depth of the board on the left. Proceed along the gap between the boards only the distance of the turn-in. Do not crease on the bare adhesive. Hold this bone folder in place while you take another bone folder and form the indentation on the edge of the other board at the head.
    This will adhere the turn-in to the depths of the board on each side of the turn-in. Do the same at the tail.
    Be careful to keep your hand and the bone folders from touching the exposed adhesive on the remaining area of the gap between the boards.

5. Lay a scrap backing paper from the Positionable Mounting Adhesive over both the leather turn-ins. Burnish with the 3M squeegee.

6. Turn the boards over on the liner. Lay a scrap backing paper on the leather and burnish.

Inlaying Leather on the Outside of the Cover

Steps 1–6 on the previous page are for applying a single strip of leather to the outside of the boards. If you wish to inlay pieces of leather to be seen on the outside of the boards as shown below, see page 181, *Inlaid Leather on the Outside of the Cover.*

Outside view of this finished cover is a little elaborate. Seven pieces of leather were used to create the quarter leather. Two colors of kangaroo leather were used. Each piece is inlaid so that it is all on one surface. All that this entails is butting one piece of leather to the next. Inlaying leather on the outside of the cover is described on page 181.

Leathers used for turning-in at the head and tail must align. The middle leather pieces can be trimmed after they are adhered to the boards. The overhangs at the head and tail are turned-in to the inside.

Six pieces of decorative papers were used to cover the outside of the boards. These, also, are inlaid. The inside of the cover is shown on the facing page; the finished book is shown on page 207.

INSIDE LEATHER/HINGE

After forming the turn-ins the leather centered on the inside of the boards will be added. For a continuous support sewing, this is referred to as the *inside leather*. For a cased-in binding, it is the *leather hinge*. First read about optional inlaid threads or strips of leather. See: *Leather Seams,* page 85.

Inside view of a finished cover shows the leather turn-ins at the head and tail. The center leather hinge is bordered by inlaid strips of the dark leather used also on the outside of the boards. Inlaid strips of leather are described on page 88, as *Optional Inlaid Leather*.

The decorative Italian pineapple paper on the outside of the boards was cut almost twice the height of the boards. This permits the turn-ins to nearly meet in the center of the inside of the boards . The inside papers, which usually are almost the dimensions of the boards are reduced here to two horizontal strips which are 3/4 x 21/2″.

The cover is now ready for a continuous support sewing. Descriptions begin on page 129.

Dimensions of the Inside Leather Hinge

Height of the inside leather/hinge is the distance between the turn-in at the head and the turn-in at the tail, *less the height* of the optional inlaid threads or strips of inlaid leather. Cut the inside leather slightly longer and trim to the final length after the adhesive backing is added.

Width of the inside leather/hinge will end up the *same* width of the outside leather, or, the same as the turn-ins. However, cut the leather slightly wider and trim to exact width after it is applied to the boards.

1. Roll out the Positionable Mounting Adhesive on the liner. Lay the leather on it, good side up. Tack the leather lightly with the squeegee. Cut the leather from the roll as described on page 37. Burnish the backing side with the squeegee.

2. Trim a little off one edge of the height and place that edge butted to the turn-in at the head. Butt it to the optional inlaid thread or strip of leather, if used. See: *Leather Seams,* page 85.

    The leather will overlap the turn-in at the tail or the optional inlaid thread or strip of leather. Find the left edge of the turn-in at the tail with the inside leather still overlapping the turn-in. If you inlaid thread or a strip of leather, find the top left edge of this instead of the turn-in.

    With the point of the #11 blade of your X-Acto knife, stab the inside leather to mark where the finished height of the inside leather will be. Do the same on the right side .

3. Remove the inside leather to the self-seal mat. Carefully line up the straightedge with the two incised marks. Trim the finished height of the leather. Place it in position on the boards to make sure it is a perfect fit.

Finishing Covers when Casing-In

The leather hinge is trimmed to finished height, but the width is left wider than needed until after casing-in. Leave the adhesive backing on the hinge. Set the case aside until after the sewing is completed. Proceed to Casing-In, page 111 and sew the book block to the hinge. After casing-in, see: *Covering the Remainder of the Boards with Paper,* page 93.

In addition, you should read *Leather Seams,* page 85 before cutting for your hinge. If you decide to inlay threads or strips of leather between the turn-ins and the hinge, your leather hinge will be cut that much shorter in height, that is, by two thickness of the items you are inlaying.

Finishing for a Continuous Support Sewing

For a continuous support sewing, the cover is finished with the following steps prior to sewing:

1. See: *Leather Seams,* page 85 to determine if you want optional inlaid threads or strips of leather before you cut the inside leather.

2. Cut the finished height, only, of the inside leather. Peel the backing. Lay it in position. Stroke the leather with the palm of your hand to tack it down. Place a scrap piece of backing paper over the leather. Squeegee lightly at first, then firmly. Never squeegee directly on the leather.

3. Trim the excess width of the inside leather and any optional inlaid threads or strips of leather to the width of the turn-ins.

4. Cover the remainder of the boards. See: *Covering the Remainder of the Boards with Paper,* page 93.

Amount of Leather Turned-In for Continuous Support Sewings

MINIMUM TURN-INS: Turn-ins should extend on the inside of the board no less than 3/4″ to make sure they adhere.

MAXIMUM TURN-INS: Turn-ins at the head and tail for a continuous support sewing can extend as far in as you wish; it is only a matter of design. For large turn-ins, see page 52. This is because sewing the section/s to the cover can take place through the turned-in leather as well as through the inside leather between the turn-ins. I suggest the turn-in be no less than 5/8″ to 3/4″ and preferably 1″as the minimum.

A turn-in of 5/8″ would make an overhang of 3/4″ at each end prior to turning-in, a total of 11/2″ for the head and tail. Some length is lost because of the depth of the board.

Height of the leather for the outside of the boards would be the height of the board plus 11/2″.

The turn-ins might extend up to 3/4″ in from the head and the same in from the tail. This would require an overhang of 7/8″ at each end.

Height of the leather for the outside of the boards would be the height of the board plus 13/4″.

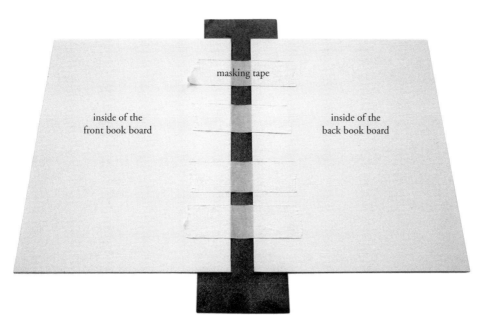

After the leather is applied to the outside of the boards, flip the boards over onto PMA Liner or a scrap piece of PMA backing paper. The leather will be on the table against the liner as shown above. The masking tape is removed so the spine paper and end cords can be added before turning in the leather.

Add the spine paper. See page 76 and illustration below.

End-cords are now set in place as shown below. Also see page 75. The turn-ins can now be made at the head and tail.

REFINING THE AMOUNT TURNED IN: Often I want the turn-ins to extend to a precise position on the board. This is because I have pre-determined the location of the sewing stations. Since I may have inlaid strips of leather on the outside of the boards I do not want a sewing station to accidentally pierce through close to the slit between pieces of leather. The stations are designed to be centered in thin strips of leather.

Edges of the turn-ins and inlays of leather on the inside must also take into consideration where the holes will be pierced. Secondly, I try to avoid butting leather on the inside of the board in the same position as on the outside. This would line up slits on the two leathers causing a weak spot.

To decide precisely where the turn-ins will extend on the inside of the boards I place scrap pieces of the PMA backing on the turn-ins before bringing them around to the inside of the boards temporarily.

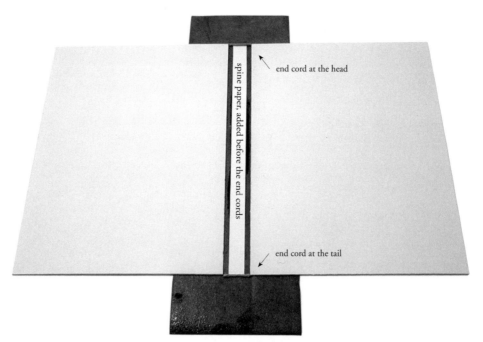

end cord at the head

spine paper, added before the end cords

end cord at the tail

Add the spine paper then the end cords before forming the turn-ins. It is dangerous to attempt trimming the turn-ins after the are attached. You might cut through the leather on the spine. Check they are cut at a right angle, and you can refine the amount turned-in as described above.

In this manner I can hold the turn-in tight against the inside of the board without it sticking to the board. Pencil lines on the board tell me the position of the sewing stations from top to bottom. Using an X-Acto knife, I stab slightly on the edge of the turn-in to mark where it needs to be trimmed. The cover is laid on a self-seal mat and the stab mark is lined up with the grid on the mat. The adjusting cut is made. The temporary scrap of backing is removed from the leather and the turn-in is formed.

ADDING THE INSIDE LEATHER: Optional inlaid threads or strips of leather are applied. The remaining inside leather/hinge is now ready to be added. Leave the backing on the leather. Butt the leather to the turn-in at the head, or to any optional inlay. With your knife, place a mark on the lower left of the leather where it meets the leather or inlaid thread near the tail. Do the same on the right. Remove the inside leather to the self-seal mat. Line up the metal straightedge with the incised marks and trim.

Set the inside leather in place on the board to see if it fits snugly. If so, remove the backing and apply the leather to the board. Finish the inside of the boards by adding the inside papers.

The cover is finished; pierce the sewing stations on the spine and the book block. The continuous support sewing can now be done.

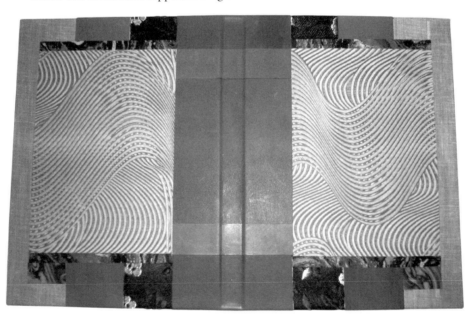

Inside of the boards is completed. This is the cover shown at the top of page 63. After the turn-ins are made on the spine, inlaid strips of leather are added before the leather hinge is adhered. See page 88. Note the brocade and strips of leather from the center of the boards were turned-in, but not extended across the inside.

TURN-INS WITHOUT SPINE PAPER OR END CORDS

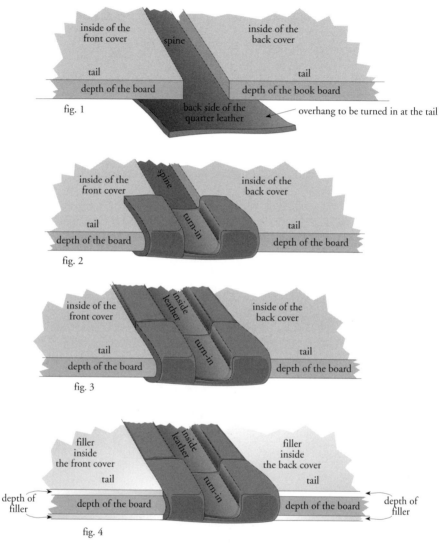

Use of filler on the boards is optional. The cover will have a 3-ply cover if filler is needed to bring the surface on the inside and outside of the board up to the height of the unpared leather. The decorative paper may be as thick as the leather and no filler will be needed.

If used, the outside filler is sanded on the foredge then covered with decorative paper.

The hinge for a cased-in book is attached to the boards after it is sewn with the book block. For a continuous support sewing the *inside leather* is applied to finish the cover before sewing. *Spine paper,* page 76, is not illustrated above. I recommend spine paper be added in the gap between the boards prior to end cords and forming the turn-ins.

END CORDS

A length of 5- or 6-ply cord can be placed horizontally the width of the spine at the head and tail prior to turning-in the leather. This gives a thickness to the spine at the head and tail. If spine paper is used, it is added before the end cords. See: *spine paper,* page 76.

The book block extends only to the end cords and tight against the inside leather so that the end cords hide a small portion of the book block looking straight down at the head or tail of the closed book. The end cord gives a finished look to the book block much as do endbands.

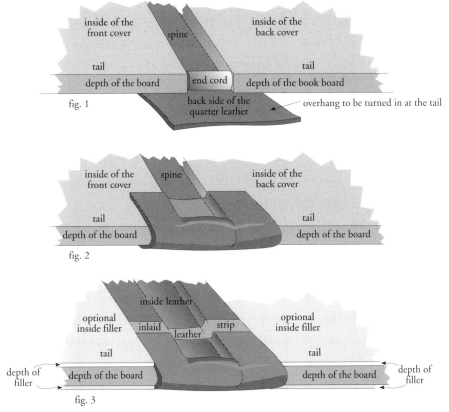

END CORDS: In figure 1 a 6-ply cord which is as long as the gap is wide is placed at the tail. Another cord is placed at the head. End cords can be used with or without spine paper.

Figure 2, the leather is turned-in at the head and, as shown here, at the tail. A bone folder creases the leather along the depth of the turn-in and the width of the gap along the cord to give shape to the end cord.

If filler is used, it is now attached to the inside and the outside of the boards ready to add decorative papers. Filler is described on page 93.

Photo illustrations of end cords are on pages 88–90.

SPINE PAPER

TURN-INS WITH A REINFORCED SPINE: A spine paper is recommended to reinforce the spine for sewing, prior to adding the end cords. I recommend Tyvek. See step 1 below.

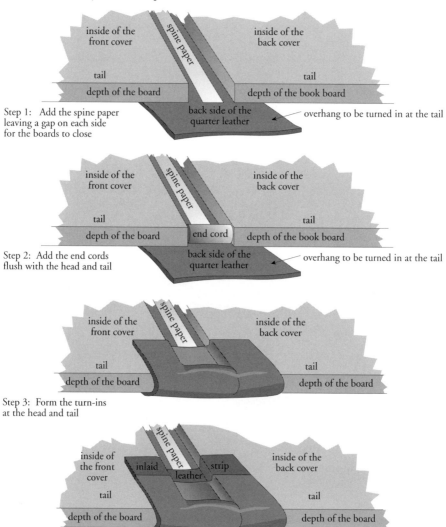

Step 1: Add the spine paper leaving a gap on each side for the boards to close

Step 2: Add the end cords flush with the head and tail

Step 3: Form the turn-ins at the head and tail

Step 4: Add the optional inlaid thread or inlaid leather strip.
Then, the inside leather/hinge for continuous support sewings will be added.

The cloth or leather spine should be reinforced for sewing. Width of the spine paper should not extend to the boards, but leave space for the depth of the board and thickness and of the leather for closing the covers. Height of the spine paper is the height of the boards.

Thin spine paper gives the leather the look of a rounded spine. A thicker paper gives a flatter looking spine. I recommend that you always reinforce the spine with a strip of paper prior to turning in the leather because in continuous support sewings you are sewing through the leather spine.

•If you are sewing one of the bindings where the thread proceeds to the head then wraps around the head to the inside, the spine needs to be reinforced with a thick paper so the wrapping of the thread will not crimp the leather at the head and tail of the spine.

• If the quarter leather is inlaid, strength of a continuous strip of leather is lost. Spine paper, especially Tyvek, connects strips of inlaid leather on the spine and hinge for strength.

Amount of Leather Turned-In for Cased-In Books

The turn-ins at the head and tail of a cased-in book must extend on the inside of the board no less than 1/2″ but *no more than 3/4″*. For a 1/2″ turn-in, the overhang must be 5/8″ because of the depth of the board.

Height of the leather for 1/2″ turn-in at the head and the tail would be the height of the board plus 1 1/4″ to account for the depth of the boards.

A small turn-in for a cased-in binding is necessary because structurally sewing of the sections must take place close to the head and tail. Since the sewing stations must also go through the hinge, the length of the hinge must be as long as possible. With larger turn-ins, the hinge would only exist in the center of the sections.

If the sewing only took place on this shorter hinge, the book block would not be attached to the case near the head and tail and would tend to be unstable.

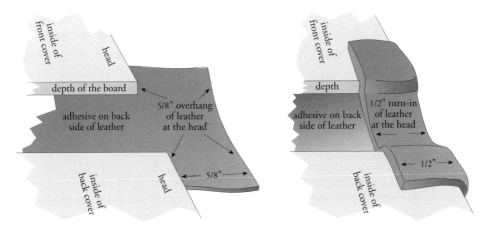

The overhang must be approximately 1/8″ longer than the amount of turn-in desired because of the depth of the board. Spine paper is not needed if you are casing-in, but end cords would be nice.

AVOIDING LEATHER WHICH IS TOO THICK

When Volume V was two-thirds finished I taught a workshop for Tom and Cindy Hollander at Hollander's School of Book and Paper Arts in Ann Arbor, Michigan. I did not take time to bind up a sample using their leathers; the students paid a price. It worked out well for me, however, because I saw two problems when the leather is too thick: *gap size* and *thickness of the fillers* .

Gap Size

When the leather is thicker the gap must be increased to accommodate the closing of the boards. See illustration on page 77. However, the solution is not to increase gap size but to use thinner leather which has been purchased shaved to 0.5mm. thickness—no thicker than Stonehenge paper. Normal leathers purchased from a bindery supply are generally three times that thickness, even though they appear fairly thin. They are inappropriate for the binding procedures described in this book.

Thick Fillers

Even if you were to broaden the gap to accommodate a thick leather, filler required to bring the surface of the board up to the height of the leather would be as thick as the book board itself.

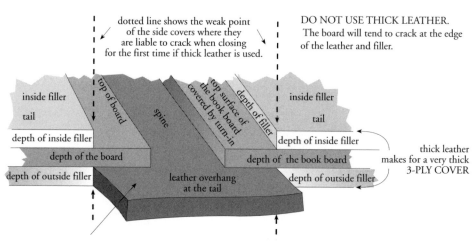

dotted line shows the weak point of the side covers where they are liable to crack when closing for the first time if thick leather is used.

DO NOT USE THICK LEATHER. The board will tend to crack at the edge of the leather and filler.

inside filler

top of board

top surface of the book board covered by turn-in

depth of filler

inside filler

tail

spine

tail

depth of inside filler

depth of the board

depth of the book board

depth of inside filler

thick leather makes for a very thick 3-PLY COVER

depth of outside filler

leather overhang at the tail

depth of outside filler

turn-in has been peeled back to show the fragility of the book board when the fillers are so thick to accomodate leather which is too thick

Thick leather requires filler just as thick and on both sides of the book board. This makes a proportionally thick, stubby cover. Worse, it is unsound. The cover is liable to crack from head to tail where the leather meets the filler. Avoid thicker leathers.

In effect, at the foredge you would have three book boards laminated, the center book board and two others used as filler. Only the center board would be at the spine edge, along with the leather turn-ins and the leather hinge. The point where the leather meets the filler on the side covers would be a weak point or fault line. See illustration to the right and on the following page. Using force to close the cover for the first time with thick leather is liable to crack the core book board.

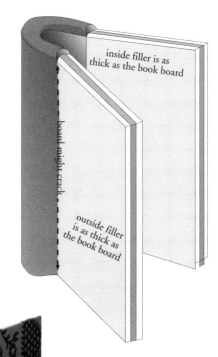

inside filler is as thick as the book board

board might crack

outside filler is as thick as the book board

ABOVE: Thick leather requires thick filler. The center board is very thin in comparison and susceptible to cracking.

Use of filler on the boards is described on page 81.

LEFT: Using 2–ply mat board or the thinnest book board is required for the bindings in Volume V.

If you purchase leather which has been shaved to 0.5 mm thickness, no fillers will be necessary.

This cover has inlays of contrasting colors of kangaroo leathers. This looks like it would be difficult to do, but it is not. It is described on page 181. Also, see: *Optional Inlaid Leather,* page 88.

LEATHER BULGE AT THE HEAD AND TAIL

Filler on the surface of the boards raises the surface of the decorative paper up to the level of the leather. However, leather going around the head and tail makes that part of the cover taller.

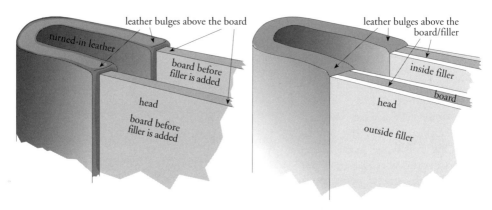

Thin leather will bulge slightly above and below the board when it is turned in. I do not mind this. You can remedy it if you wish by *Notched Boards* or *Filler on the Edge of the Board* as explained below.

Optional Notched Boards

In *Bookbinding for Book Artists* the solution was to notch the boards in the area where the leather is turned in, recessing the leather so it is the same height as the rest of the boards. This is tricky and I always cut the notch too deep so my leather fell below the remainder of the board. It is difficult to cut to the exact depth needed. In this volume I do not notch the boards.

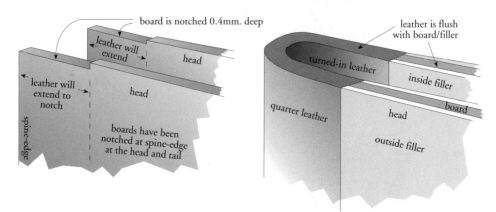

OPTIONAL: Notch the boards at the head and tail slightly less than the thickness of the leather. Be very careful. Too deep a notch will recess the height of your leather.

Optional Filler on the Edge of the Boards

Filler can wrap around the depth of the board to adjust the height of the side covers to the height of the leather when it is turned in. If one piece of filler is used, it is nearly impossible to measure the exact height of filler needed to circumvent both sides of the board. The seam should cross the center of the board, as it may show when decorative papers are added.

Any approach to adding filler to the depth of the board requires agility. If you insist on eliminating the leather bulge, I suggest using two fillers. Cut each to the required width. Height is the height of the cover plus the depth of the board. Score and fold the two fillers.

Positionable mounting adhesive will not stick to edges of the boards. PVA glue must be used in order for the filler to adhere to the depth or edge of the board.

One filler is glued. It is positioned at the head on the outside of the board and extends across the depth of the board at the tail. To avoid warpage, immediately glue the filler for the other side of *this* board. Apply it to the inside of the same board starting on the inside at the tail. This filler will cover the depth of the board at the head.

After the glue has dried, sand the seams. Slightly sand the outside of the filler at the foredge to taper the side cover. Notching boards and filler is described in case you want to use either. I use thin leather. I do not notch the boards. I do not use fillers.

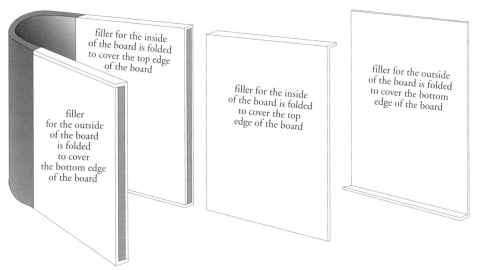

OPTIONAL: Filler for the edge of the board is achieved by scoring and folding the filler for the board so that it extends across the depth of the board. One filler can cover the depth at the head while the other covers the depth at the tail. PVA glue must be used in order for the filler to adhere to the depth of the board. After the filler is added and the glue has dried, sand the seams. Slightly sand the outside of the filler at the foredge to taper the side cover. Any use of filler is unnecessary, unless you insist upon it.

The first few prototypes I made for Volume V continued the use of fillers started with *Bookbinding for Book Artists.* However, I quickly eliminated the use of fillers. My leather is extremely thin and hardly bulges above the surface of the paper/s on the outside of the boards. And I am, after all, trying to make quick bindings.

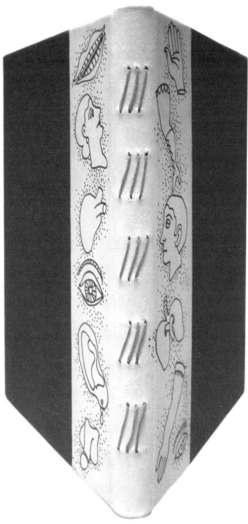

Shan Ellentuck, pen and ink drawing of milagros on quarter kangaroo leather. The sewing is Hash Marks, described on page 253. 13.5 x 10 x 1 cm.

Bindings from Volume V were tried out on students at Penland School, in June 2002. Shan prefaced showing me her sewing of the book pictured above with a story:

A lady decided to make a unique Easter dinner. In an old French cookbook she found a recipe for a ham terrine. It had dozens of ingredients and required special equipment, but she decided to make it anyway. After hours of measuring, mixing, chopping, stirring and cooking, she carefully turned the terrine de Jambou out onto a platter as her husband looked on. Then she sliced into the end to taste her masterpiece—and burst into tears. "Oh honey," she cried, "I've made Spam!"

Shan thought her quarter leather endeavor was such a let down, but she was too harsh on herself. It is a lovely book and several people visiting the classroom were drawn to it.

LEATHER SEAMS

When leather is pared thinly and overlapped using wheat paste, seams are hardly noticeable. Butting unpaired leather to leather leaves a noticeable seam which tends to look unfinished. This is a problem I had to deal with in adding the inside leather tangent to the turn-ins at the head and the tail. It is the same problem as casing-in the leather hinge tangent to the turn-ins.

The following are three solutions for giving a finished look to the seams:

1. The least favorable way is to PVA a thin strip of decorative paper over the seam as part of your design for the inside of the boards.
2. Better, inlay a 4-ply color linen thread in the seam prior to adhering the inside leather or hinge. See page 86.
3. Best, inlay a thin strip of contrasting color of leather. See page 88.

DECORATIVE PAPER OVER SEAMS

I do not care for this approach because I do not like the interruption of the vertical leather up the spine. It is a makeshift solution, unless you can design it better so the paper strip looks intentional.

This is an example of paper glued over the seams on the inside of a quarter leather cover using PVA.

OPTIONAL INLAID THREADS

When I first showed an unpared leather binding to the Association of Book Crafts in Auckland, New Zealand, in May 2000, one of the members of the guild came up with a good solution for the seam between the leathers. I wrote down her name and promised to credit her. Unfortunately, I have misplaced the note.

At least I can say inlaid thread is not my idea, but one of those fine New Zealanders with whom I worked. This is her solution:

A contrasting color of thread is inlaid between the turn-ins and the inside leather. One thread is between the inside leather and the turn-in at the head, one thread inlaid between the inside leather and the turn-in at the tail. Or, inlay two threads at the head and two at the tail as in the illustration below. Also, look at the illustrations on pages 48–51.

After forming the turn-ins, step 4, page 67, the thread are adhered to the boards:

1. Cut two threads which are about an inch wider than the leather turn-ins, one for the head and one for the tail.
2. Place wheat paste on your forefinger and thumb. Stroke one thread to coat it. Slightly untwist as you coat with paste and then replace the twist.
3. Place the thread in position, tightly against, but not overlapping the turn-in at the head. Center the thread extending beyond the leather on both boards.
4. Press it into place with a bone folder but do not smash the thread. Diameter of the thread should remain close to the thickness of the leather. Press the thread down the depth of both board edges. Make sure the thread is tangent to the leather across the entire width of the turn-in.

   Coat the second thread with paste and apply to the boards tangent to the turn-in at the tail. Allow to dry.

Four threads were inlaid in this example, two at the head and two at the tail, shown in this detail of a quarter cloth binding.

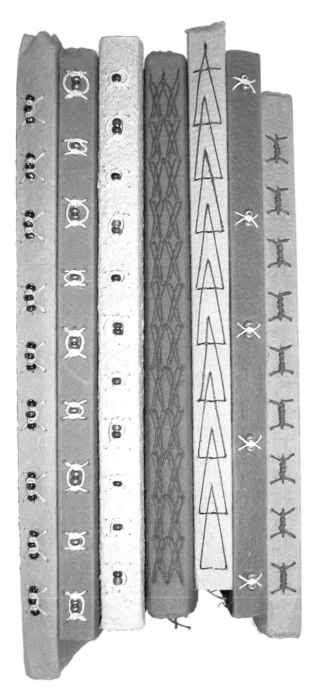

Catherine Tedford and Carol Mathey, binding samples from Non-Adhesive Binding Volume II *1–, 2– & 3–Section Sewings.* Cathy is director of the Richard F. Brush Art Gallery, St. Lawrence University. Carol is the Assistant Director. In addition, the two teach binding and the book arts.

I photographed these sample bindings on 22 September 2002 at a Visual Studies Workshop weekend class conducted by Scott McCarney and myself.

The bindings to the left use hand made papers with saturated color as the covers. The paper, along with strong color in the thread and beads make for a group of exciting bindings.

Each is approximately 10 x 14".

These samples seem irrelevant to Volume V, but that is not so. Besides wanting to show this work, I want to stress that *all* the 122 sewings described in Volume II can be translated to hard cover, quarter leather, using PMA to attach the leather and decorative papers to the boards.

OPTIONAL INLAID LEATHER

March 10, 2002. I inlaid threads on a quarter leather cover. Since the color thread was pre-waxed, I used PVA rather than wheat paste. It was nearly impossible to keep my sticky fingers off the leather and I got some glue on the turn-in. That was enough to prompt me to find a new solution for the seams.

This solution is exciting to me. It does not use paste or glue, so it is quick and I can't mess up the job nearly as easily. Use your scraps of adhesive-backed leather cut to thin strips. Adhere them to the board tangent to the turn-ins instead of inlaying thread. It looks great.

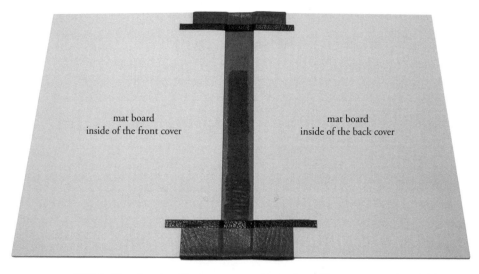

mat board
inside of the front cover

mat board
inside of the back cover

STEP 1: Place the strips of leather tangent to the turn-ins making sure to press them tightly to the depth of the boards with a bone folder.

1. Form the turn-ins. Cut thin strips of contrasting leather which has been backed with adhesive. Place one strip below the turn-in at the head on the left board, only. Press the strip down the depth of this board with a thin bone folder. Continue to lay down the strip across the gap between the boards, tangent to the turn-in.

    Place one bone folder on the strip against the left board. With a second bone folder, press the strip up the depth of the right board. If you do not hold the strip in place on the left board the strip could pull away from the depth of that board while pressing against the depth of the right board. Place the remainder of the strip on the right board tangent to the turn-in.

Press downward firmly on the strip of leather with a bone folder but do not stroke the leather. The strips of leather should be tangent to the turn-ins. Be sure to press tightly to the depth of the boards with a bone folder.

2. Measure the inside leather/hinge. This is described on page 69. Trim the height only of the inside leather/hinge. Check to see it fits.

FOR CONTINUOUS SUPPORT SEWING: Peel off the backing and place the leather on the board as shown below. Continue to step 3 below.

FOR A CASED-IN BINDING: Do not peel off the backing. Sew the book block to the hinge first. The case-in as described on page 111.

STEP 2: Measure the inside leather. Use a slightly long piece of adhesive-backing leather. mark and trim the height as described in step 2. Adhere the leather to the board now, unless it is for a cased-in binding. I have used the exact width needed for the inside leather. You may use a wider piece and trim it along with the strips of leather.

3. Lay a straightedge along the left turn-in at the head and tail. Trim off the excess width of the hinge and the leather strips. If you made the inside leather wider than necessary, it will be trimmed, as well. Do the same on the right board.

    Measuring the inside leather the finished width is a little dangerous as it might not be quite wide enough. Better to make it wider and trim it down to the same width as the turn-ins.

4. *OPTIONAL FILLER:* If filler is used, place it on the board tangent to the leather. Check to see if it is the proper thickness, i.e. the same as the leather.

I do not use fillers. If you wish to do that, cut four fillers, one each for the inside and outside of the left board and for the right board. Trimming the filler and sanding the foredge is described on page 94, 95. Apply the filler to the board. Cover the filler with decorative papers. See: *Covering the Remainder of the Boards with Paper,* pages 93–101.

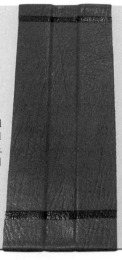

Leather hinge and strips
of inlaid leather
are trimmed the width
of the turn-ins.

The cover is mat board.
If filler is needed it will be added
now, so the decorative paper will
reach the thickness of the leather.
Difference in levels is not critical
on the inside of the boards.

Leather hinge and strips
of inlaid leather
are trimmed the width
of the turn-ins.

The cover is mat board.
If filler is needed it will be added
now, so the decorative paper will
be flush with the thickness of the
leather. Difference in levels is not
critical on the inside of the
boards.

STEP 3, above: Trim the strips of leather and hinge the same width as the turn-ins.
STEP 4, below: Add the 4 pieces of filler to the inside and outside of the boards.

Filler is added,
if desired, to bring this area
of the inside of the board
flush with the leather.

Filler is added,
if desired, to bring this area
of the inside of the board
flush with the leather.

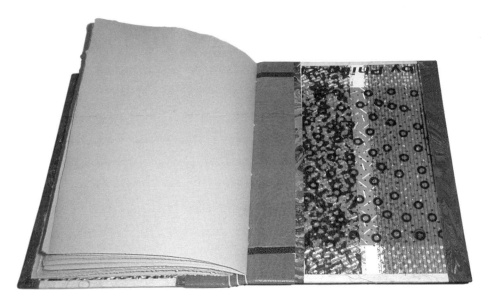

This is the inside of the cover after the decorative papers are added and the book block has been sewn. The book is finished. Other pictures of this binding are on pages 21, 263, 269–271.

For inlaying leather on the outside of the boards, see the description on pages 181–183 and page 204.

COVERING THE REMAINDER
OF THE BOARDS WITH PAPER

The remainder of the outside of the boards will now be covered. The following description is for a single decorative paper, one for each board. If you wish to inlay several papers, see: *Inlaid Papers,* page 117.

OPTIONAL FILLER

Before the papers for the outside and inside of the boards can be applied a filler paper could be added to the four bare surfaces of the boards:

the outside of the back cover

the outside of the front cover

the inside of the back cover

the inside of the back cover

See the illustrations on page 74 and 94.

Thickness of the Filler

If you order the kangaroo leather, request it shaved to 0.5mm thickness. Unpared leather is easier to use when it is this thin and you *will not need filler* if the thin leather is near the thickness of the paper for the board. All outside surfaces of the finished cover ideally are the same level, free of ridges.

1.   *FILLER FOR THE OUTSIDE OF THE BOARDS:* Select a blank white paper to use as a filler. The kangaroo is approximately the thickness of BFK Rives and Stonehenge, archival papers ideal as the filler. Without cutting the filler to size lay it on the board tangent to the leather. Place the decorative paper on top of this. Run your finger back and forth across the paper and leather to see if they are on the same level.

If there is a ridge up to the leather, select a thicker paper as filler. If there is a ridge up to the level of the papers, select a thinner paper as the filler.

2.   After you have selected the proper thickness of paper to use as filler, trim the filler slightly larger than the bare surface of the board. Cut a second piece the same dimensions for the outside of the other board.

3.   Roll out the Positionable Mounting Adhesive on the liner. Lay the two filler papers on it as described on page 36. Tack the papers lightly with the squeegee. Cut the fillers from the roll as described on page 37. Burnish with the squeegee.

4.   Do not peel off the backing but cut each filler to the precise size of the bare area of the outside of the boards. Lightly mark the fillers with pencil to keep track which is which. If you are like me, your covers may vary slightly in size.

5. Remove the backing and carefully attach the fillers. Make sure the filler butts to the leather. Check to see if there is any overhang where the filler extends beyond the boards. If so, lay the boards with the filler side down on the self-seal cutting mat.

    Trim the excess filler to the edges of the head, foredge and tail. Be careful not to cut the leather or to trim away any of the board. I find that pushing down and slightly forward with a single edge razor blade keeps from cutting into the depth of the book board.

6. Turn the boards with the filler side up. Lay a scrap sheet of backing paper over the filler and leather. Burnish the fillers to adhere them permanently to the boards.

QUICK FINAL TRIM: Here is a quick method for determining the final trim size of the filler: Lay a straightedge of the adhesive-backed filler on the board, tangent to the leather and the tail. Turn the cover over onto a self-seal cutting mat keeping the filler in position. Place the point of your #11 X-Acto blade against the edge of the board at the head near leather. Pierce through the adhesive/filler to make an incised mark.

Do the same along the head at the foredge. Pierce incised marks at the edge of the board on the foredge—pierce close to the head and one close to the tail.

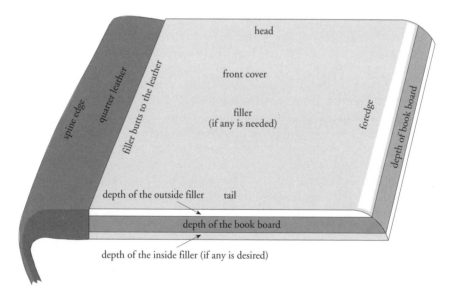

STEP 8: Sanding the foredge of the book gives a finished feel to the foredge. The sanding illustrated above is to an extreme bevel. Do not sand off so much that you weaken the cover at the foredge.

Set the cover aside. Turn the filler over on the cutting mat. Line up the straightedge with your incised marks and trim the filler. Apply the filler to the outside of the board.

7. *FILLER FOR THE INSIDE OF THE BOARDS:* Repeat Steps 2–6 above to cut and adhere the fillers on the inside of the boards.

8. Lightly sand the foredge of the front and back outside fillers, only. This will take the sharpness off the edge. If no filler is used, sand the boards. You might prefer to bevel the foredge for a pronounced tapering, as shown on the previous page. The foredge feels smooth and "finished" when holding the book.

PAPER FOR THE OUTSIDE OF THE BOARDS

1. Measure the decorative paper which will cover the outside of the boards. *Height* of the paper is the height of the boards plus the overhang at the head and the tail which is generally 3/4″ at the head and 3/4″ at the tail. Total of both overhangs is 11/2″. The height of the paper will be the height of the boards plus 11/2″. Cut the paper slightly larger than needed. It will be trimmed to exact dimensions after the adhesive backing is attached. *Width* of the paper is the width of the bare area of the board plus an overhang of 3/4″. Measure from the leather to 3/4″ beyond the board. Cut the paper slightly larger to be trimmed later.

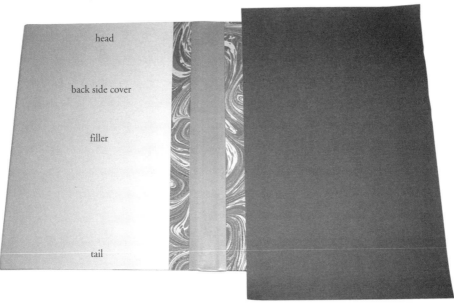

Applying the adhesive-backed paper to the board. Strips of marbled paper have already been adhered and turn-in, butted to the leather.

Cut a second piece the same dimensions for the other board.

In the picture on the previous page, strips of marbled paper were adhered to the outside of the boards tangent to the leather. These were turned in to the inside of the boards.

The large, dark, laid paper covering the remainder of the outside board was then butted to the marbled paper strip.

As stated in Step 6 on the facing page, after the paper is placed on the front of the board, lightly squeegee it to tack it down. Turn the boards over on the liner to trim the corners. *Cutting Off the Papers at the Corners:* Trim the corners at the foredge as shown above and described on the facing page as step 1. Use an X-Acto knife, not scissors.

2. Roll out the Positionable Mounting Adhesive on the liner. Lay the two decorative papers on it with the good sides facing up. Tack the papers lightly with the squeegee. Cut the fillers from the roll. Burnish with the squeegee.
3. Trim the papers to the finished dimensions stated in step 1.
4. Remove the backing and carefully attach one of the decorative papers. Make sure the paper butts to the leather. The cover should be on the liner paper so the overhang will not cling to the table top.
5. Lay a scrap sheet of backing paper over the decorative paper and leather. Burnish lightly. Run your finger along the edges of the board to slightly crease or score the paper showing the outline of the board. Make sure the overhang is not pressed down against the liner.
6. Turn the board over. Paper at the corners will be trimmed on a self-seal mat with an X-Acto knife as the paper would stick to scissors.

FORMING THE PAPER TURN-INS

1. *CUTTING OFF THE PAPERS AT THE CORNERS:* An overhang of the outside paper is about 3/4 to 1″ along the head, tail and foredge. The excess paper at the corners must be removed.
Cut the corners of the paper at about a 45° angle.
Amount of paper removed must be exact: the cut is out from the board, leaving a paper margin which is 1 1/2 times the thickness of the board.
Position of the cut is critical. If your diagonal cut is too close to the board, the bare board will be exposed at the corner when making the turn-in. If the cut leaves too much paper at the corner, you will have an excess of paper when folding the outside paper around to the inside of the board.
2. *MAKING THE TURN-INS:* Fold the paper around the tail, tight against the edge of the board, onto the inside surface of the book board. Push with your thumb on the paper in the direction towards the head. This will tighten the paper on the edge of the board as well as on the inside. Lightly burnish with the squeegee.
Do the same at the head. Fold the paper around the head, tight against the edge of the board, onto the inside of the board. Push with your thumb towards the tail. Burnish with the squeegee.
3. Place the board on the table with the inside of the board facing up. Place the bone folder flat against the edge of the board at the tail, close to the foredge. Take the bone folder tightly around the corner onto the foredge, with the bone folder flat against the edge of the board. This creases the paper at the corner. Do the same at the head.
4. Turn in the paper along the foredge. Press it tightly over the edge of the board onto the inside of the board. Press in a stroking manner toward the spine-edge to tighten the paper.

Lay the bone folder over the seam at the corners on the inside of the board. Press downward to crease and flatten the paper.

Repeat Steps 1–4, *Forming the Turn-Ins* on the other side cover.

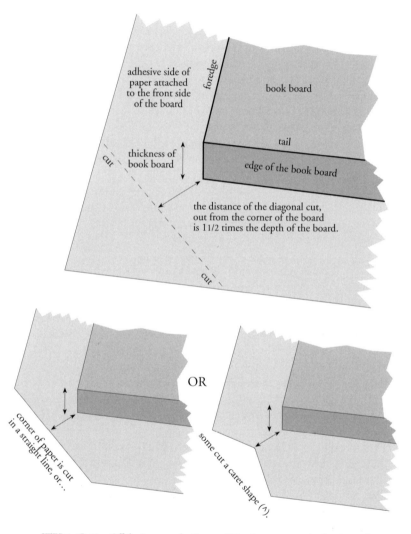

STEP 1, *Cutting Off the Papers at the Corners:* Trim the corners at the foredge as shown above and described on the previous page as step 1. Use an X-Acto knife on a self-seal cutting mat.

Do not attempt cutting with scissors. The adhesive would stick to the scissors and tend to tear the paper. It took me months to understand that and see how easy this step is with a blade and you can be so much more accurate, too. My mind was stuck in the wheat paste mold of cutting off corners.

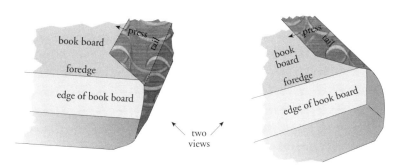

STEP 2: Folding in the paper around the tail is described on page 97.

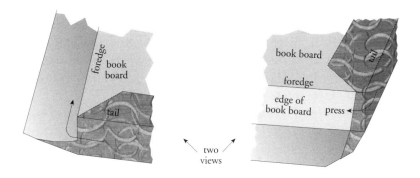

STEP 3: A bone folder is used to tuck in the extra paper.

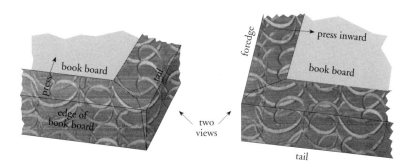

STEP 4: The paper is turned in along the foredge.

ADDING THE INSIDE PAPERS TO THE BOARDS

Prior to sewing the book block to the cover, covering the boards for a continuous support sewing is completed at this point by adding the inside papers.

For a cased-in book, the inside papers cannot be added until the book block is cased-in with the hinges. This is because the width of the hinges must be trimmed to the width of the turn-ins before the inside papers can be added.

NOTE: In my other volumes, the inside papers are referred to as *island paste-downs.* Since no paste is being used in this volume, I will refer to this as the *inside papers.*

To add the inside papers, these are the steps:

1. *Height* of the inside paper has some leeway. It must overlap the turn-in of paper at the head and tail. Generally leave about 3/16″ of the turn-in paper showing along the head and the same amount at the tail. That means the height of the inside paper is the height of the board, less 3/8″.

    Cut the height of the inside paper slightly larger. It will be trimmed to the finished height after the adhesive backing is added.

2. *Width* of the inside paper has the same amount of turn-in paper from the front of the boards showing along the foredge on the inside of the board. Width of the inside paper is measured from the inside leather to the foredge of the board, minus the amount of turn-in to be left showing. Since the height of the inside paper allows 3/16″ of the turn-in paper to show at the head and tail, the same amount will be permitted to show along the foredge. Therefore, the width of the inside paper will be the distance from the inside leather to the foredge, less 3/16″.

    Cut the width of the inside paper slightly wider. It will be trimmed to the finished width after the adhesive backing is added.

3. Roll out the Positionable Mounting Adhesive on the liner. Lay the inside papers on it, good side up. Tack them lightly with the squeegee. Cut the papers from the roll as described on page 37. Burnish the papers lightly with the squeegee.

4. Trim the inside papers to the finished height and width on a self-seal mat. Remove the backing paper from one of the inside papers.

5. Place this paper in position on the board tangent to the inside leather. Light squeegee the paper to tack it down.

6. Place a scrap piece of backing paper over the inside paper. Squeegee lightly at first, then firmly. Do the same with the other inside paper.

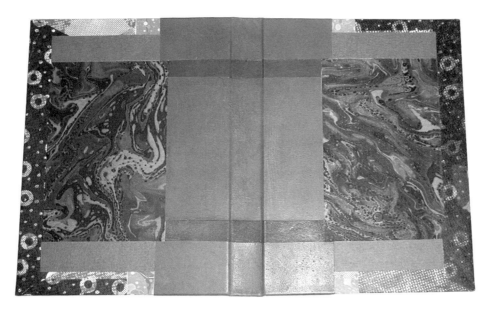

The inside papers have been added above. The marbled paper on the inside is bordered by strips of laid paper above and below. Inlaid strips of leather are between the turn-ins and the inside leather. This is a cover for a small sketch book designed to fit in a shirt pocket. The finished book was given to Aatis Lillstrom. I want to see if the cover will be durable.

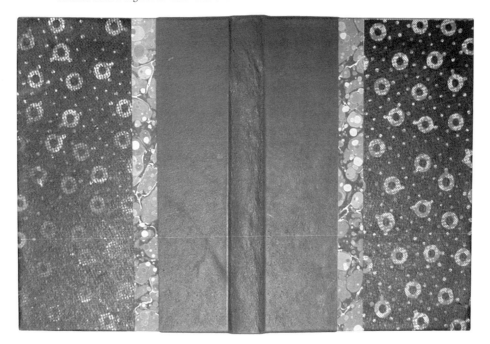

MARKING STATIONS ON
A LEATHER SPINE

Designing the Stations for the Spine

Design your stations on a scrap paper to the dimensions of the spine. Rule off vertically the space needed for the boards to close. The template will be the width of the spine-gap, less 3 thicknesses of board to permit the covers to close.

If you are going to do several bindings, print out a couple pages of templates on your computer. Stations can be marked on the templates lightly in pencil. You can erase and adjust the position of your stations This speeds up designing stations for the spine.

Sample templates appear on pages 106 and 107. These can be photocopied; nothing is printed on the verso of the templates. If you wish to take a knife to this book, you can cut them out—the prospect of which kind of gives me chills.

Better, draw your own templates on the computer slightly taller than the height of your future books. Save the templates as a document to be printed out when needed.

Each of your printed templates is cut out and trimmed to the height of your boards. A number of templates are needed, each for differing number and varying thickness of the sections.

Piercing the Stations on the Spine

Never design or mark sewing stations directly on a cloth or a leather spine. It is unsightly. Make a template. Place the paper template directly onto the inside of the cover, centered on the spine. Carefully holding the template in registration, pierce the stations.

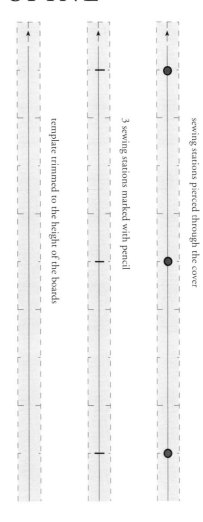

template trimmed to the height of the boards

3 sewing stations marked with pencil

sewing stations pierced through the cover

Printed templates can be ruled off from head to tail. Vertically, a line is printed for each section of the book block. This is for a 1-section 3-hole pamphlet sewing.

Students in Ann Arbor who tried out some of these bindings pre-publication complained the template slipped and their holes did not line up.

Masking Tape Template

To insure no slippage when piercing the spine, place a strip of masking tape the width and length of the spine on the inside of your cover. Do not press firmly, as you do not want to leave a residue of adhesive on the leather or book cloth. Transfer the measurements from the template to the tape.

Better, use white artist's tape because it is not as sticky as masking tape. It comes is 1/2″, 3/4″ and 1″ widths which makes it is ideal for use without having to trim the width. Pierce the stations through the tape then remove the tape.

You should still take the time to design the placement of the stations on a template, especially for multi-section sewings.

NOTE: Test the tape on scrap leather. It may scar or discolor leather.

Artist's Tape is white and a little less sticky than masking tape. It is ideal as a template temporarily attached to the inside of the spine. It comes in various widths so it only has to be trimmed to the height required.

The stations are pierced through the tape and leather, then the tape is removed.

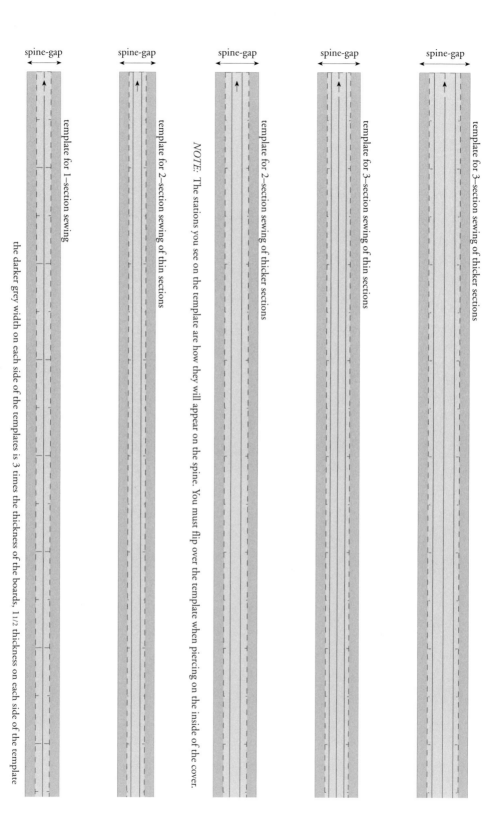

spine-gap

spine-gap

spine-gap

spine-gap

spine-gap

template for 1–section sewing

template for 2–section sewing of thin sections

template for 2–section sewing of thicker sections

template for 3–section sewing of thin sections

template for 3–section sewing of thicker sections

NOTE: The stations you see on the template are how they will appear on the spine. You must flip over the template when piercing on the inside of the cover.

the darker grey width on each side of the templates is 3 times the thickness of the boards, 1 1/2 thickness on each side of the template

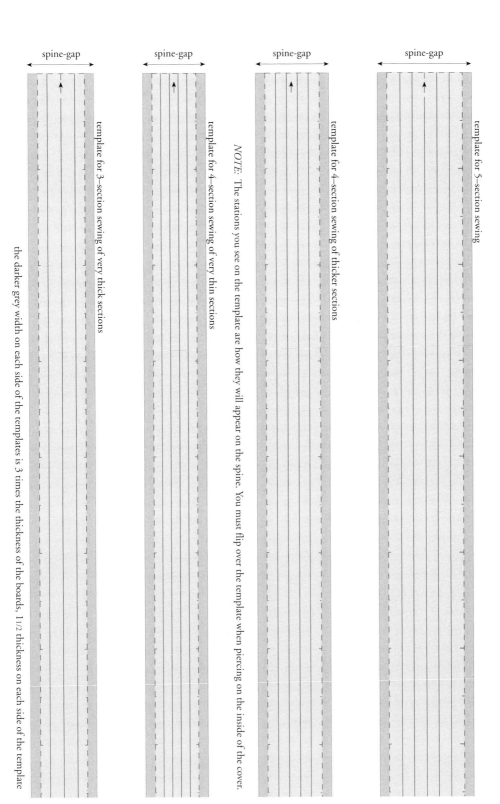

spine-gap

spine-gap

spine-gap

spine-gap

template for 5-section sewing

template for 4-section sewing of thicker sections

template for 4-section sewing of very thin sections

template for 3-section sewing of very thick sections

NOTE: The stations you see on the template are how they will appear on the spine. You must flip over the template when piercing on the inside of the cover.

the darker grey width on each side of the templates is 3 times the thickness of the boards, 1 1/2 thickness on each side of the template

Adjusting a Template

Positioning the stations vertically can be adjusted easily. Sometimes I have spaced the stations nicely but find I have too much space between the head and the first station and too little space between the final station and the tail.

Rather than calculate the measurements again, I just adjust the template a little higher on the spine. This saves a lot of time since designing the stations is time consuming.

Design of the stations is achieved, but placement from head to tail is inferior, as there is too little space between the final station and the tail.

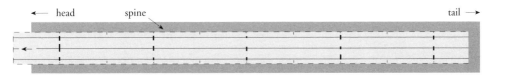

Rather than measure all the stations again on a new template, the original template is simply shifted to achieve a better position on the spine.

Reversing the Template

Draw your design of the position of the sewing stations on the template. This is the view from the outside of the spine. Remember to flip your design over when you place it on the inside of the spine to pierce the stations. Otherwise your design will be backward on the outside of the spine.

NOTE: All the sewing stations diagrammed in my books are for the outside of the spine. You must reverse your template when piercing from the inside of the cover.

CASING-IN

INTRODUCTION

When I started writing this book I thought that Position-able Mounting Adhesive would be a great solution to casing-in. I had planned to show single and multi-section book blocks cased-in using PMA on the hinges.

Now that I have completed the writing of Volume V, I am re-writing this chapter. I have reduced casing-in with PMA to describing only one binding, and it is limited to a single section.

In a cased-in book, the only thing that holds the book block in the covers is the adhesive connecting the two. Either the first page is glued to the boards, or, better, a hinge of cloth or leather attaches the book block to the boards. It is critical that the adhesive holds.

I do not think that PMA has the sticking power of PVA glue, so I do not recommend casing-in a book block of more than a single section with PMA. Secondly, it is just a little more difficult to line up the hinge tangent to the turn-ins with the book block attached to the hinge.

The benefit of this binding, along with the Exposed-Spine Board, page 157, is that there is no sewing exposed on the spine. Instead of drawing with color thread stitches you are free to draw on the leather with a bone folder, pen and ink or watercolor.

A 1-section cased-in codex with indented drawing on the quarter leather.

If a multi-section book block is to be cased-in, use PVA glue, not mounting adhesive.

Procedure

On a book cased-in with PMA, the leather hinge must be cut and the adhesive backing added to the hinge prior to sewing. Do not remove the backing from the hinge until after pamphlet sewing the section to the hinge.

1. *Temporary Height* of the hinge is cut slightly longer than the distance from the leather turn-in at the head to the tail on the inside of the board. It will be trimmed to the exact height in step 4.

2. *Temporary Width* of the hinge is cut about 1″ wider than the turn-ins. It will be trimmed down to the exact width of the turn-ins only after the book block and hinge are sewn and the book is cased-in by attaching the hinge to the boards.

Steps 7–9 on the facing page: A sleeve of wax paper is placed around the book block with the hinge protruding. This will protect the pages from creasing as you case-in. It will also free your hands to align the hinge to the case. The sample above is not the same book shown on the previous page.

Mark an arrow for *up* on the masking tape to prevent casing in the book upside down. Peel the backing off the hinge and attach it to the boards.

Step 14: Above, the book block is shown cased-in and the hinges trimmed. The adhesive can be seen where the excess hinge was peeled away. The inside papers will be added next.

3. Roll out the Positionable Mounting Adhesive on the liner. Lay the leather hinge on it, good side up. Tack the leather lightly with the squeegee. Cut the leather from the roll as described on page 37. Burnish the backing side with the squeegee.

4. *Finished Height* of the hinge is cut before sewing. Place the hinge on the inside of the case, lining up the top left corner of the hinge with the bottom left corner of the turn-in at the head. If you are using the optional inlaid threads or leather strips, line up the hinge tangent to the inlaid item. Mark the hinge on the bottom left side where it meets the turn-in at the tail, or where it meets the thread or inlaid leather. This mark should not be pencil, but an incised line as small as you can make and still see it. The cut will be more precise than a pencil dot and will not be seen in the finished book.

   Line up the hinge at the top left on the front board at the bottom of the turn-in at the head, or at the bottom of any inlaid thread or leather. With an incised cut, mark the hinge at the bottom left where the hinge meets the turn-in at the tail, or where it meets any inlaid item.

   Theoretically this should be the same height as the other mark if you have true 90° cuts on all the leather turn-ins and the hinge. I often do not. This insures the leather will fit perfectly.

5. On the self-seal mat, line up the straightedge with the two incised marks. Trim the hinge to the finished height, but leave the excess width for now. *Do not peel* the backing off the leather until after the hinge and book block are sewn and you are ready to case-in.

6. Sew the hinge to the single section book block with a pamphlet sewing, page 159, making sure the book block is centered on the hinge.

7. Place a wax paper sleeve around the book block, but leave the hinge outside the sleeve. The sleeve should be the same width as the book block so that it is easier to handle. Seal the sleeve with a couple pieces of masking tape. Mark the masking tape with an arrow to show which end is up to prevent casing in the book upside down.

   The sleeve will protect the pages from being creased and free both hands for casing-in.

8. Open the case and place it on the table. Peel the backing off the hinge. The paper backing will rip as it passes each stitch, but will probably come off in one piece.

9. Carefully position the book so the hinge is tangent to the turn-ins at the head and tail, or tangent to the threads if optional inlaid threads are used. Make sure the book block is centered on the spine.

10. Lightly press the hinge onto both boards. Set a couple books as a support on the back board. Lean the book block against the support to free both of your hands.

11. Run a bone folder on the hinge, along the spine edge of the front board. Hold the book block in a vertical position. With the bone folder still in position along the edge of the front board, use a second bone folder to crease along the spine edge of the back board. Allow the book block to rest against the support.

12. Place a scrap of backing paper over the hinge on the front board. Squeegee firmly. Move the book support to the front board and rest the book block against it.

13. Place a scrap of backing paper over the hinge on the back board. Squeegee firmly.

14. *Finished Width of the Hinge* is the same width as the turn-ins. Trim the hinge and any optional inlaid threads or leather strips at this point: Place a metal straightedge on the board lined up with the turn-ins at the head and tail. Trim off the excess width of the hinge and any inlaid items. Remove the straightedge to peel away the excess hinge and inlays, if any. Trim the hinge on the other board in the same manner.

15. Now the inside papers can be added to complete the binding. Follow steps 1–6 of *Adding the Inside Papers to the Boards,* page 100.

NOTE: After you try this approach to casing in, the next time I suggest you cut the hinge to the finished width *before* sewing. It is risky because the hinge might not line up perfectly with the turn-ins if you are not careful. However, if you find it easy to do, this will save steps in trimming twice and avoids the cuts in the board.

Inside view of the front cover shows the tan leather hinge cased-in tangent to the wine-colored leather turn-ins. The inside paper, from Hollanders, is printed in metallic ink.

CASED-IN CODEX: The book block is a single section, pamphlet sewn to the leather hinge, backed with positionable mounting adhesive.

Turn-ins at the head and tail are wine colored kangaroo. Center leather is a pinkish-tan. A drawing has been embossed into the leather, left blind with no ink. Horizontal ink lines border the drawing.

INLAID PAPERS

COLLAGE: Using several papers you can create a collage on the boards. If several papers are designed for the outside of the boards, they must not overlap. Otherwise, when the book is placed on and removed from the shelf, edges will tend to catch and peel back or tear. The papers must be inlaid, all on the same surface, all the same thickness. If your collage is on the inside of the boards, levels of papers pose no problem.

Each piece of paper for the collage should be backed with adhesive prior to cutting. There is some leeway in sliding and butting together pieces on the board, but not nearly as much ability to be adjusted as when inlaying with pasted papers.

IMPROMPTU: The design is almost always pre-planned, but can be improvised, placing contingent pasted pieces side by side until the board is covered. The design shown on the following pages is pre-planned, as generally that is the approach.

EVEN OVERHANG ON ATTACHED BOARDS: When improvising a design on the outside of the board for a quarter leather binding, the touching papers must overhang at the head, tail and foredge to be used as the turn-ins. The design will butt up against the quarter leather.

PREPARATION

TOOLS: A thin bladed knife is needed. I use an X-Acto™ knife with #11 blades. Use a new blade for every inlay cut. The once-used blades can be used later for less critical cutting.

A self-seal cutting mat is an ideal surface, if not mandatory, for cutting inlays. Using book board is perilous. When the blade crosses a previous cut, the diverging blade will cause a disaster.

HOLDING THE KNIFE: In cutting two layers of paper at once for an inlay, keep the blade perpendicular to the cutting surface or the bottom paper will be a different size. With adhesive backed paper, this requires cutting through four layers with a single stroke. This is slightly more difficult, but not as much as you might think.

Angle of the blade is important to prevent rough edges. I hold mine rather steep for better results. The angle is no more than that shown on the following page. Start at the head, beyond the papers, cut through to beyond the tail, making the curve as well as insuring severing both sheets.

PRE-BACK THE PAPERS: Back all the papers with the adhesive. Do not peel off the backing until all the pieces are ready to be attached to the board.

CUTTING THE PIECES

Designs with Rectangular Pieces

If the design consists of butting rectangular pieces together, make your design and cut all the pieces to the final dimensions. Remember that pieces which are at the edge of the board must extend approximately 3/4″ beyond the edge to be used as the turn-ins.

STRAIGHT CUTS: Use a metal straightedge and X-Acto knife with a #11 blade to cut the pieces. After cutting, arrange the design to check for fit. Make sure you allow for the turn-ins on the head, tail and foredge.

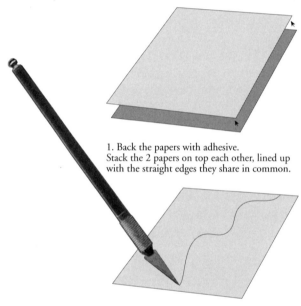

1. Back the papers with adhesive. Stack the 2 papers on top each other, lined up with the straight edges they share in common.

2. Make a single cut through both papers with a new blade. Keep knife perpendicular to self-seal cutting mat.

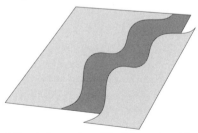

3. Use the larger piece of the lighter color with the smaller piece of the darker. The back cover could use the leftovers, with the design in reverse colors.

Designs with Curves

Curves cannot be cut separately or the shapes will never line up tangent.

INLAY CUTS: The two tangent papers must be cut simultaneously so the curves are identical and the seams will butt consistently

1. Back the papers with adhesive. Lay the adjacent curved pieces on top of each other making sure the bottom piece is large enough for the shape.
2. Cut the curve of both papers, the concave and the convex , in a single action. There are no second chances. See drawing on the facing page.

CHECKING THE DESIGN: Once all the paper has been backed and cut to the finished dimensions place them on the cover next to the quarter leather *without* removing the backing. Butt them together to check your design. Make sure you left an even overhang along the head, foredge and tail.

APPLYING THE PIECES TO THE BOARD: Remove the pieces from the board. Arrange the design beside the cover. Place the cover on the liner.

1. Pick up the piece that is the largest and which butts against the quarter leather and overhangs the board. Remove the backing from this one piece only. Position it on the board and tack it down with the squeegee. All other shapes will be positioned by this first key placement, so be very careful it is aligned perfectly.
2. Pick up the adjacent piece which is tangent to the leather. Peel off the backing and add it to the board. Tack it down.
3. Continue in this manner until all pieces which are tangent to the leather are adhered to the board. Then add the pieces, one by one, which are tangent to the ones on the board, working your way towards the pieces which overhang the foredge.
4. When all pieces adhered to the board check the overhang. If it is not perfectly even the overhang can be trimmed now or after the turn-ins are made. If you choose to trim on the inside of the board after turn-ins are completed, see the procedure in step 6 on the following page.

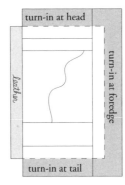

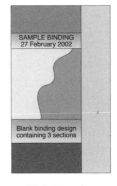

1. line drawing for cover

2. drawing with turns-in

3. assembled pieces of cut papers backed with adhesive

4. quarter leather case with inlaid papers on the front board

TO TRIM OVERHANG BEFORE MAKING THE TURN-INS: Take the board to the self-seal cutting mat. Place the design face down so the exposed adhesive of the overhang is face up.

Lay a narrow scrap backing paper over the overhang which is to be trimmed. Place your straightedge over the backing paper and trim the overhang.

5. *CUTTING THE CORNERS:* See: *Cutting Off the Paper at the Corners,* page 97. Make the turn-ins carefully to maintain all the seams butted on the edge and the inside of the board. See page 99.

6. *TO TRIM OVERHANG AFTER MAKING THE TURN-INS:* Unlike inlaying pieces using wheat paste, I prefer to trim the overhang after the turn-ins of all the pieces are completed. This will insure an even turn-in. Hold the straightedge in place after making the cut and peel away the excess. Even tiny slivers can be removed, whereas if the papers were wet with paste, the cuts would probably tear the papers. This is an area where the adhesive backing is superior.

INSIDE PAPERS: The inside papers are added now if the cover is for a continuous support sewing. If this is a cased-in binding, the inside papers will not be added until after the book block is sewn to the hinge, the book is cased-in and the hinge has been trimmed.

Quarter leather 3-section sewing with papers inlaid using the adhesive backing method described. 24.5 x 15 x 2.2 cm.

NOTE: In step 3, page 119, you cannot assemble the cut shapes and place them on a single sheet of the positionable mounting adhesive. When the backing is peeled, the pieces will individually fall to the table. Adhesive may extend from the edges of the pieces. Each paper must be backed separately with PMA *before* you cut the shapes.

 PEELING OFF THE BACKING: Peel off the backing only on the piece you are about to apply to the board. Then peel the backing from the next piece and apply to the board. If you mistakenly peel the backing from leather or paper before it is needed, place the piece on a scrap of backing with the sticky side towards the backing. This will protect the adhesive until you are ready to apply that piece to the board.

Quarter leather prototype with inlaid papers using 568 Positionable Mounting Adhesive to apply the leather and papers. 19 x 14.5 x 1 cm.
For inlaying leather on the outside of the boards, see description on pages 181–183 and page 204.
For inlaying leather on the inside of the boards, see *Optional Inlaid Leather,* page 88.

STAGES OF MAKING
A 2-BOARD COVER

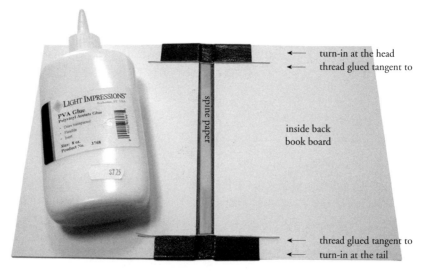

turn-in at the head
thread glued tangent to

inside back
book board

thread glued tangent to
turn-in at the tail

Determine the gap, page 64. Add the outside leather. Add spine paper, end cords and make the turn-ins, pages 74–77.

Add the optional inlaid leather strips. See page 88. In this description optional threads will be inlaid with PVA glue tangent to the turn-ins as described on page 86.

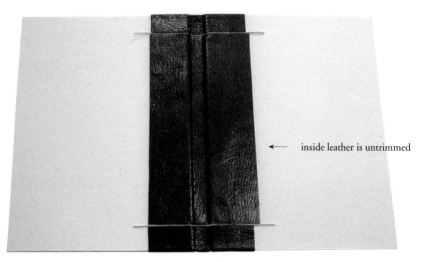

inside leather is untrimmed

Measure the inside leather tangent to the threads and wider than the turn-ins, page 69.
Cased-in books do not add the hinge until after sewing is completed, page 111.

NOTE: I recommend you reinforce the inside of the spine with a strip of paper before forming the leather turn-ins. See: *Spine Paper,* page 76.

inside leather and inlaid threads have been trimmed leaving a little bit of the suede on the board

Trim the inside leather and optional threads or inlaid leather strips the same width as the turn-ins, page 89. Notice the suede has stuck to the board when the excess leather was peeled away. For trimming the width of the hinge of a cased-in book, see page 70.

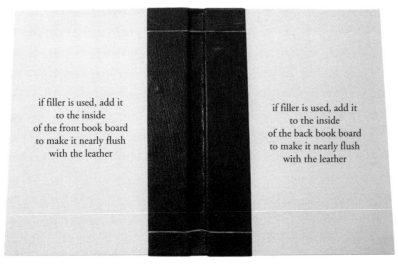

if filler is used, add it to the inside of the front book board to make it nearly flush with the leather

if filler is used, add it to the inside of the back book board to make it nearly flush with the leather

Measure and add the filler to the remainder of the inside board for the front and back covers, if you decide to use fillers. See page 93. Filler will be the near the height as the leather. The addition of decorative paper brings the surface flush with the leather.

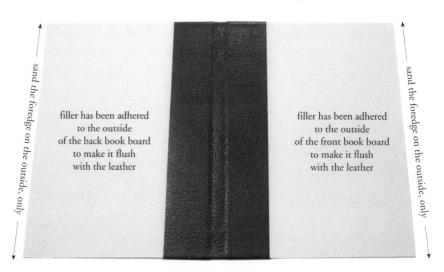

sand the foredge on the outside, only

filler has been adhered
to the outside
of the back book board
to make it flush
with the leather

filler has been adhered
to the outside
of the front book board
to make it flush
with the leather

sand the foredge on the outside, only

Measure and add the filler butted to the leather on the outside of the boards, page 93.
Sand the foredge of the outside of the boards, only. See pages 94, 95.

1-Section Sewing
FAUX DOUBLE RAISED CORDS
Devised 28 February 2002

Paper is added to the outside of the boards. Here, two sheets are cut the same size simultaneously to form an inlay. See page 118.

On a self-seal cutting mat the two papers are layered and cut at once. In this example I use half the pieces for the outside of the front cover and the leftovers for the back cover.

Inlaying starts with the piece/s tangent to the leather. One piece at a time is added to the board. See page 119.

The papers are backed with adhesive prior to cutting. Piece by piece the papers are butted to the board and turned-in to the inside.

The final paper is added to the front board. It is turned over and the corner cut to form the turn-in. The inlays are added to the outside of the back board.

This is the completed view of the outside of the cover. Pictures of this book are on pages 17, 142, 143 and 146.

The inside papers are added to finish the cover. Wood veneer was onlaid with strips of laid paper. Papers on the inside of the boards can be *onlays,* rather than inlays, since the surface does not have to maintain a single level as on the outside of the boards.

CONTINUOUS SUPPORT SEWINGS

INTRODUCTION

All but one sewing are sections sewn directly to the spine of the cover, which functions as a continuous support. I will devise several sewings starting with a single, two, three, sections (signatures) and proceed from there. I used to plan out books. Now, they just kind of evolve.

It is important to offer sewings of a different number of sections. This will present a range in the number of pages from which to choose for a particular project you have in mind.

Originally I was going to simply copy and paste text descriptions of sewings from Volume II for this book. But I thought, "What the heck, they already have access to those descriptions. If they want to transpose those sewings to hard cover or quarter leather, they can do that on their own. Why not give them some new ones?"

Actually, that is not quite true. I wasn't thinking of offering more to my readers, I was thinking of myself. If I am going to make all the dozens of prototype attempts at leather bindings needed to write this book, I want to entertain myself with bindings I have never done before. So, I decided to make up new sewings for Volume V.

I looked at the 1-section sewings in Volume II on my bookshelf. All had vertical stitches since the sewing runs along the single section down the spine-cover. I thought, "Why not try horizontal stitches!" *1-Section Faux Single Raised Cords* is the first. Looking at the closed example, the horizontal threads across the leather remind me of raised cords. Of course there are no cord supports in this structure. Compare this to the 1-section sewing described on page 141—same idea. The title *Faux Double Raised Cords* is my attempt at humor.

Sewing through leather gives a sturdier support than sewing through a paper cover, so I can take advantage of that in the horizontal stitched designs.

I am fond of the stitching seen on the inside of the boards, as well. See illustrations on pages 54, 146, 147, 150, 151 and 160.

One reason for writing this book is my love of books containing a single section. I don't want to see them relegated to magazines or even booklets with paper covers, as in Volume II. Hard cover and even a quarter leather spine and leather hinges on the inside makes a substantial physical object.

A good number of my own artist books need no more than a single section. I think you, too, will have use for these single section *books*—I won't call them booklets.

SEWING POSITION

Many sewings are simplified by sewing on the bench (laid on the table). These sewings are easier sewn by standing the cover in front of you, the section/s behind the cover.

1-SECTION

FAUX
SINGLE RAISED CORDS

If hard covers and quarter leather isn't enough to dress up a book, then what more? I guess raised cords. So with a smirk this was my first sewing for Volume V. It started me off on horizontal stitches on the spines of these bindings and I haven't recovered as of the date of this writing.

PREPARATION

Compile one section (signature) with the outer folio/s laid paper as the endsheets. Measure the bulk. See: *Determine the Gap between the Boards,* page 64.

Make the cover, finishing both sides of the boards. Read pages 61–83.

Sewing Stations

The leather spine will have 3 holes at each station. One hole on the cover will be in the gutter, tangent to the spine edge of the back board, one in the gutter tangent to front board. The third hole will be centered between stations *A, B* and *C.*

Determine how many sets of stations are desired on the spine. Drawing the stations on the inside leather would be unsightly. Cut a scrap paper the height of the cover and as wide as the gap. Measure and mark the stations on the scrap paper. When satisfied, position the paper carefully in the gap between the boards on the inside of the cover. Hold in place and pierce the stations in the cover.

Place the section in position in the cover. Mark the stations on the fold of the section with a pencil. Pierce the stations.

1-Section Faux Single Raised Cords with 7 sets of stations.

135

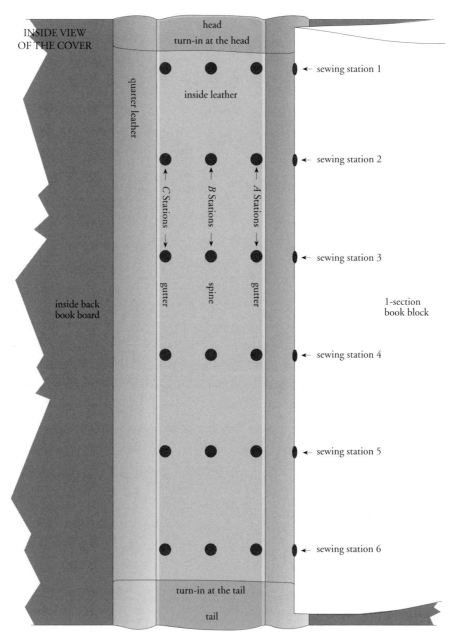

SEWING STATIONS: The sewing will be described with 6 stations on the book block. The cover will have 6 sets of stations with 3 holes each to align with the book block.
NOTE: On the inside of the cover, the stations are left to right: *C, B* and *A.* On the outside of the cover, they read left to right: *A, B* and *C.*

The description utilizes 6 sets of stations. This requires 6 holes in the section and 18 holes in the leather on the spine.

A STRANGE PAMPHLET SEWING: If you follow the pathway in the drawing to the right you will see it is basically a 3-hole pamphlet sewing at each set, minus the ties-off. The difference is the pamphlet sewing is horizontal, not vertical. Something about avoiding vertical stitches on the spine must be going through my brain these past few weeks of devising sewings.

Directing You to a Particular Hole on the Spine

As an example, the station at the top left is 1*A*. The middle station in the second set is 2*B*. The right station at the tail is 6*C*.

SEWING PROCEDURE

1. Start inside the section. Take the needle out station 1 of the section and station 1*B* of the cover. Leave about 8″ of thread inside the section. Proceed on the spine to 1*A*. Enter the cover, only.

2. Proceed in back of the section, from underneath the thread extending from the section to cover. Exit the cover to the outside at station 1*C*. Adjust the thread so there is about 4″ thread inside the section. Tighten the horizontal stitch on the spine. Make it taut, but do not distort the leather.

3. Enter the cover and the section at 1*B*.

4. Tie a square knot on the inside right at station 1. Clip the shorter thread to about 1″.

5. Proceed towards the tail to the next section. Exit the section and cover at the *B* station.

6. Proceed on the outside to the *A* station. Enter the cover, only.

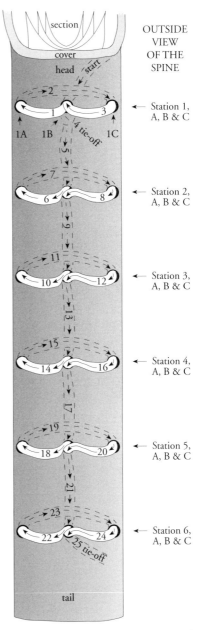

OUTSIDE VIEW OF THE SPINE

← Station 1, A, B & C

← Station 2, A, B & C

← Station 3, A, B & C

← Station 4, A, B & C

← Station 5, A, B & C

← Station 6, A, B & C

STEP1: The sewing starts inside the section and exits the section and the cover at Station 1*B*. The thread spans and enters the cover, only, at 1*A*. Steps 2, 7, 11, 15, 19 and 23 do not enter the section.

137

7. Proceed on the inside of the leather, under the sewing, to the *C* station. Exit through the cover.
8. Proceed on the outside to the *B* station. Enter the cover and the section.

Sewing the Remaining Sets of Stations

Repeat steps 5–8 for each set of stations. Upon completing step 8 on the final set of stations, tie-off with a half hitch.

NOTE: Steps 2, 7, 11, 15, 19 and 23 enter the leather, only, at the *A* stations then cross the spine and exit the *C* station. They do *not* enter the sections.

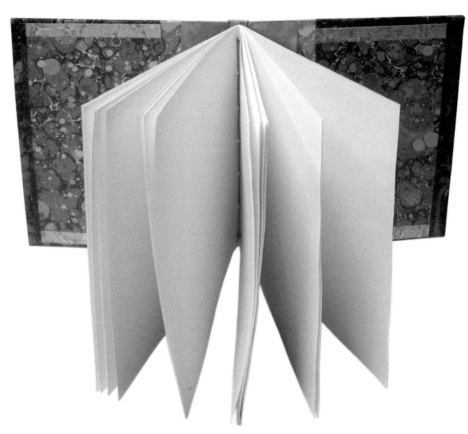

FAUX SINGLE RAISED CORDS: This sewing shows a single thread on the inside of the middle of the section.

This single section sewing uses kangaroo for the quarter leather cover.

Faux Double Raised Cords, 1-section sewing.

FAUX
DOUBLE RAISED CORDS

PREPARATION

Compile one section with the outer folio/s laid paper as the endsheets. Measure the bulk.

Make the cover, finishing both sides of the boards. See: *2-Board Covers,* pages 61–83.

2-NEEDLE SEWING: This is a 2-needle sewing which means using one thread with a needle on each end.

Sewing Stations

The leather spine will have 2 holes at each station. One hole on the cover will be in the gutter, tangent to the spine edge of the back board, the other will be in the gutter tangent to front board. Viewed from the outside, the left hole is station *A.* The right is station *B.* See page 143.

Determine how many sets of stations are desired on the spine. Don't draw the stations directly on the inside leather. Cut a scrap paper the height of the cover and as wide as the gap. Measure and mark the stations on the scrap paper. When satisfied, position the paper carefully in the gap between the boards on the inside of the cover. Hold in place and pierce the stations in the cover.

Place the section in position on the cover. Mark the stations on the fold of the section with a pencil. Pierce the stations.

This example is sewn with one color of thread.

The sample described has 5 sets of stations. This requires 10 holes in the cover and 5 holes in the section which align vertically with the holes in the cover.

TWO COLORS OF THREAD: Since you have to keep track of two needles, referred to as the *a* thread and the *b* thread, it is easier if your first attempt at sewing this is done with two colors of thread. It will be easier to keep track of which needle is which. Actually I prefer using two colors of thread. The sample to the right uses a 3-ply lighter thread and a 4-ply darker thread. The lighter thread appears almost as a highlight on the spine.

Choose two contrasting colors of thread. Tie the two threads together using a half *K* close to the ends of the thread. Clip the ends so there is little thread extending from the shorter ends of thread. Place a needle on the two longer pieces of thread.

SEWING PROCEDURE

1*a* Set aside the section. Start inside of the cover, only. Take one needle, referred to as the *a* thread, which is lighter in color, out station 1*A* onto the spine. From the outside view, shown on the facing page, exit on the left of the spine.

1*b* Take the other needle, referred to as the *b* thread, out station 1*B*. Looking at the outside view of the spine, exit on the right. Center the dangling threads on the outside. If you are using two colors of thread the knot will be centered inside of the cover.

Stand the book and turn it around so you are looking at the cover from the outside. The *a* thread and the *A* stations are on the left, The *b* thread and *B* stations on the right. Set the section in position.

2*a*, Pick up the needle of the *a* thread which is extending on the outside from station 1*A*. Proceed on the spine to 1*B*. Enter the cover.

3*a* Proceed to and enter the section at station 1 from the mountain peak to the valley.

2*b* Pick up the needle of the *b* thread. Proceed on the spine to 1*A*. Enter the cover through the same hole in the cover, but below the *a* thread.

3*b* Loop thread 3*a*. Enter the section at station 1 from the mountain peak to the valley. Pull the stitches on the spine taut. Make them parallel and tangent. As you adjust the threads, keeping the section centered on the spine.

4*a* Proceed with the *a* thread inside the section towards the tail to the next station (station 2). Exit the section to the right, onto the inside of the front board. Exit the cover out the *A* station. Pull the thread outside.

4*b* Proceed with the *b* thread inside the section towards the tail to the same station the *a* thread exited (station 2). Exit the section, only, also to the right. Pull both threads on the inside the section taut.

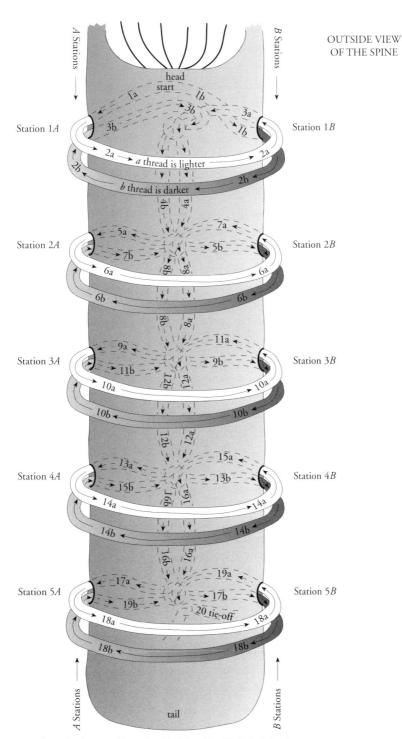

Sewing pathway for the 2-needle sewing titled Faux Double Raised Cords.

While holding them taut, take the needle for the *b* thread and loop around the *a* thread (in the gutter on the inside of the right board). Proceed under the section below the *a* thread to the left board. Exit the cover out the *B* station. Pull the thread to the outside. Keep the section centered on the spine. Looking at the outside of the spine the *a* thread dangles from station 2*A*. The *b* thread dangles from station 2*B*.

NOTE: Looping with the *b* thread in steps 3*b* and 4*b* will remove the tension from the paper at the station in the book block. This will prevent the hole from enlarging in size as the pages are turned.

5*a* Pick up the *a* thread extending from the *A* station. Proceed across the spine to the *B* station. Enter the cover, only, above the *b* thread.

5*b* Pick up the *b* thread, proceed across the spine to the *A* station. Enter the cover, only below and parallel to the *a* thread.

NOTE: Always enter the cover with the *a* thread first. Keep the *b* thread below the *a* thread, tangent and parallel to it. This is especially important when using two color threads as suggested in the illustration on page 144.

6*a* Sit the book on the table with the outside of the cover on the table. The *A* stations of the cover are now on the right; the *B* stations on the left.

This example is sewn with two colors of thread.

Pull both threads down and taut so they extend below the cover, between the cover and the section. Pull the *a* thread to the right, beyond the right side cover. Pull the *b* thread to the left. This twists the thread to relieve the tension upon entering this section.

With the *a* thread enter the section at this same numbered station heading from the right to the left. You will have to dangle the right side cover off the table in order for the needle to enter the section from the mountain peak to the inside without pulling the section from the cover.

6*b* With the *b* thread enter the section at this same numbered station heading from the left to the right. You will have to dangle the left side cover off the table in order for the needle to enter the section.

Sewing the Remaining Sets of Stations

Repeat steps 4–6 at each successive station towards the tail. Upon entering the section at the final station you will tie-off:

TIE-OFF: Using one needle, loop the two stitches in the gutter (slide the needle under them.) Pull the thread taut. Using both threads tie a square knot at the final station inside the section. Clip the threads to about 1˝.

FAUX DOUBLE RAISED CORDS: This sewing has two threads on the inside of the middle of the section.

VIEW INSIDE THE COVERS

Opening the cover of the sewing referred to as Faux Double Raised Cords, the horizontal threads extend from the book block across the gutter to the hinge. These threads, which extend from the book block, exit through the leather hinge to the outside tangent to the boards. This creates a dotting of color threads as a design element.

FAUX DOUBLE RAISED CORDS: This is the completed single section sewing. Inlaid threads are seen on the inside of the boards. The horizontal threads are seen at each station in the gutter. Wood veneer is adhered as the "inside paper".

FAUX DOUBLE RAISED CORDS: This is my first sewing of this new binding, so it is less elaborate than that on the facing page. I do like opening the cover and seeing not only a leather hinge, but the dotting of color from the threads at each sewing station seen in the gutter. Less successful was the use of strips of paper PVA glued over the seams of the leather turn-ins.

LOOP-PACKED TAPES

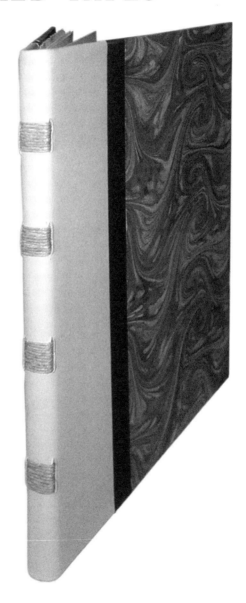

In Volume III packed cords were described. The thread loops the cord support and the coils of thread are tangent. None of the cord can be seen. This is a *loop pack* and the inspiration for this binding.

FAUX TAPES: This time I have used what might be called "tape supports". Instead of the tapes crossing and perpendicular to the spine, I have turned the supports 90° so they are parallel with the spine. In fact, they are not separate from the spine, but part of it. They are slits in the leather:

Four sets of small vertical slits were made at the hinging points on the leather. This will permit looping the thread around these portions of the spine. Thread exits the single section book block, loop packs the tape, then re-enters the section.

The series of single section sewings I am devising for Volume V seem all to have faux cords or tapes thus far and show my fascination for making horizontal stitches on the spine rather than vertical stitch-es—which are more common to 1-section sewings—and I am thinking up more such sewings all the time. Some probably will be included.

In the previous sewing, I liked opening the board and seeing the partially visible horizontal stitches in the gutter. I have played up that motif in this sewing as shown in the illustration on the following page.

Loop-Packed Tapes, a 1-section sewing in quarter (kangaroo) leather. 19 x 14.5 x 1.2 cm.

PREPARATION

Gap between the board is determined. See page 64. The quarter leather is attached to the two boards. Decorative paper is adhered to the remainder of the outside of the boards and turned in. The inside papers finish the cover.

1. Make up a 2-board cover reinforced with a stiff spine-paper. See page 76.
2. Determine the number and size of the vertical "tapes". Determine the spacing of the tapes on the spine. The description uses 4 sets of slits making 4 tapes, requiring 8 pierced sewing stations in the section.
3. Lightly mark the position of the slits in the hinge with a pencil dot on the inside leather. Cut the slits with a new blade and a metal straightedge.
4. Mark the stations on the section to align with the top and bottom of the slits. Open the section and pierce the stations.
5. Take about 3 feet of thread. Thread the needle. This is a single needle sewing.

Opening the cover not only shows a leather hinge but also the packed sewing. The blocks of horizontal stitches dot the gutter along the edge of the endsheets.

Leather hinges add a nice touch to the inside of the covers. The threads add another texture and use of color.

Only two boards were used in the cover of this first prototype with no board on the spine. It is a little difficult to sew without distorting the leather on the spine, even when the leather is reinforced with a stiff spine paper. A third board for the spine would solve this problem as in the sewing, *Exposed-Spine Board*, described on page 157 and illustrated on the facing page.

Loop-Packed Tapes is reproduced in color on the back cover of Volume V.

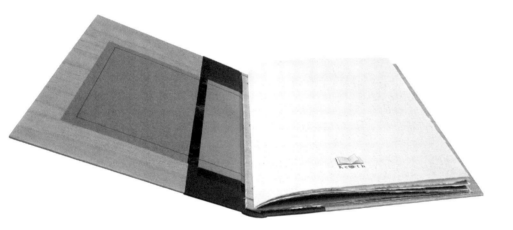

Loop-Packed Tapes can be sewn with a reinforced spine. A thin spine board made of oak tag, stiff paper or strip of metal is added in the gap between the boards prior to adding end cords and forming the leather turn-ins. See Exposed-Spine Boards, pages 58, 59 and Spine Paper, page 76.

Make sure the spine board or thin spine board does not extend to the side covers or the covers will have no hinge for the boards to close. Also, there must be space between the side covers and the spine board for the sewing stations through the leather.

A better use of a wooden or metal spine board is to expose it—not on the outside of the cover, but inside the opened book. This is described in the following sewing, *Exposed-Spine Board,* page 157.

You can read about traditional exposed-spine boards on page 57.

Sewing Stations

The sewing uses 4 "tapes" which are slits in the leather spine. This requires 8 pierced stations in the section. The pierced stations line up with the bottom and top of the slits in the cover. If you wish 5 bands of packed threads on the outside of the spine, use 5 "tapes" and 10 pierced stations.

SLIT STATIONS IN THE COVER: Cut a scrap paper the width if the gap between the boards and the height of the cover. Design the spine for the position and number of slits and and the height of each on the spine and draw these on the scrap paper. Slit the stations in the leather against the spine-edge of the side covers.

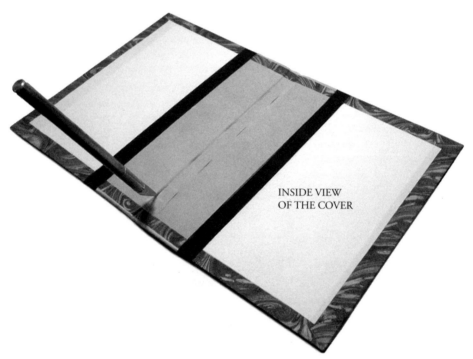

INSIDE VIEW
OF THE COVER

SLITTING THE LEATHER: Four small sets of slits are made on the inside of the cover in the gutter. This forms the vertical "tape supports" for the sewing. The eight sewing stations on the section correspond to the beginning and end of the slits.

When making the cover place a stiff spine board in the gap between the side covers before making the turn-ins. See page 76.

PIERCED STATIONS FOR THE SECTION: Place the section on the cover next to the slits and center it head to tail as shown on the facing page. Mark the stations on the section with a pencil. Remove the section and pierce the stations.

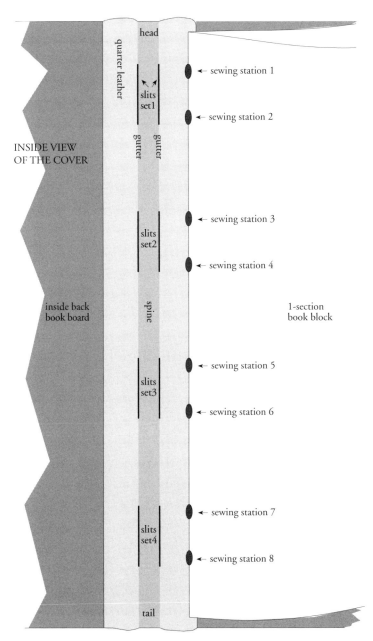

INSIDE VIEW OF THE COVER

quarter leather

head

slits set1

gutter

gutter

inside back book board

spine

slits set2

slits set3

slits set4

tail

← sewing station 1

← sewing station 2

← sewing station 3

← sewing station 4

1-section book block

← sewing station 5

← sewing station 6

← sewing station 7

← sewing station 8

SEWING STATIONS: Center the section from head to tail on the inside of the board. Place the spine fold (mountain peak) next to the slits in the leather. Place a pencil dot on the fold to mark the sewing stations on the section. The stations will line up with the top and bottom of each pair of slits on the spine.

SEWING PROCEDURE

1. Start on the inside of the section. Exit station 1 of the section. Looking at the cover from the open section, exit the left slit of the cover at the head.
   Pull all the thread through except about 6″ right inside the section. Push the exiting thread to the top of the slit.

2. Turn the cover and section 180° so you are looking at the outside of the cover. Take the exiting thread through the slit is now on your left.

3. Proceed on the outside of the cover across the spine. Enter the corresponding slit across the spine on the right next to the front side cover, but do not enter the section. Pull thread to the inside of the front cover so the stitch on the spine is taut. Adjust the stitch on the spine to the top of the slit. This creates one horizontal stitch on the spine. On the inside of the front cover, pull the thread toward the tail, then under the section to the back side cover.

4. Without entering the section, exit the left slit on the same pair of slits, just below the thread in the previous step.

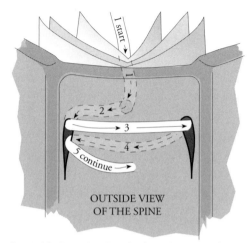

OUTSIDE VIEW
OF THE SPINE

Start inside the section. Exit the slit on the spine and enter the paired slit, but not the section.d

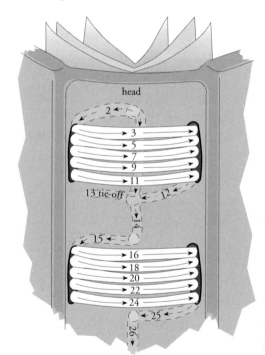

Steps 3–11 packs as many threads as needed to fill the slits (cover the "tapes").

12. Enter the cover.
13. Enter the section and tie-off with a square knot.
14. Proceed to pierced station 2 and exit.

Proceed across the spine and enter the right slit, but do not enter the section. Pull the thread to the inside of the front cover. Adjust this stitch on the spine so it is tangent to the first stitch. On the inside of the front cover, pull the thread down, then under the section to the inside of the back cover.

5–11. Exit the left slit on the same pair of slits, just below the other two stitches. Enter the cover, only on the paired slit on the right.

Proceed in this manner until you have made as many wraps to fill this set of slits. You will end up on the inside of the board. The first "tape" is now packed. The illustration shows 5 stitches on the spine as step 11 enters the cover.

Tying-Off

12. Proceed inside the cover to the section. Enter the section from the mountain peak at pierced sewing station 2.

13. Tie a square knot at station 2 with the dangling thread inside the section. Clip the shorter thread to 1/2″.

Sewing the Remaining Stations

14. Proceed to station 3. Exit the section.

15. Exit to the left on the second pair of slits. Pull thread to the top of the slit.

16. Enter the right slit of this pair of slits but do not enter the section.

17. Proceed under the section to the back cover.

18–24. Exit the left slit on the same pair of slits, just below the other stitch. Enter the cover only on the paired slit on the right. Continue in this manner until the second pair of slits contains the same number of stitches on the spine as the first pair of slits. In the illustration there are 5 stitches as step 24 enters the cover. The second tape is now packed. You will end up on the inside of the board.

25. Take the needle through the mountain peak of sewing station 4. Proceed inside the section towards the tail. Exit station 5 of the section and the left slit of the third pair of slits.

Continue sewing in this manner until all the tapes have been packed. Enter the cover then the mountain peak of the final pierced sewing station of the section. Tie-off inside the section with a half hitch.

EXPOSED-SPINE BOARD

PREPARATION

Construct a 2-board cover, with end cords, page 61–83. Use spine paper, not a spine board. Add the inside leather. See page 69 and read the chapter on *Exposed-Spine Boards,* page 57.

For books under 9 x 12″ use 2-ply mat board for side covers.

The spine board is seen only on the inside of the cover. It is not part of the cover which is completed before sewing.

An exposed-spine board on a thin book containing a single section can be made of metal. Wood is more tricky since the small piece needed might splinter. For exposed wooden spine boards use a thick single section or a book block of 2 or more sections.

Construct the Cover

SIDE COVERS: If you start with the dimensions of the cover instead of the book block, measure and cut the boards for the side covers slighter larger than the section for an overhang at the head, tail and foredge. The square of the book is generally 1 1/2 times the thickness of the board.

Width of the side covers must include the depth of the spine board, the width of the book block plus the square of the book.

The exposed-spine board is seen only on the inside of the cover. See page 160.

SPINE BOARD: After the cover is completed, a separate wooden or metal spine board will be cut to fit on the inside of the cover.

Height of the exposed-spine board is the height of the section. If you used end cords in making the cover, the height of the exposed-spine board will be measured to fit snugly against the cords at the head and the tail.

Width of the spine board is the width of the spine paper. That is, the width of the spine board leaves a gap on each side the thickness of the side cover plus 1 1/2 thickness of leather to permit the cover to close. Gap between the boards is described on page 64.

Use a Dremel Moto-Tool™ and proper bit to drill the metal or wooden spine board.

FIRST SEWING

The first sewing, a 3-hole pamphlet sewing, attaches the book block to the exposed-spine board and is hidden on the back side of the spine board.

SEWING STATIONS: Pierce 3 holes in a section, one about 1/2" to 3/4" from the head, another that distance from the tail. The third hole is centered.

Align the section with the underneath side of the spine board and mark the stations. Draw a vertical pencil line on the back of the spine board and drill the 3 holes with as small a drill bit as will accommodate your sewing needle. Make the pamphlet sewing.

Finish the inside of the cover with a leather hinge. Drill the sewing stations in the spine board.

Start on the *back side* of the exposed-spine board to hide the knot.
Clip the threads short and try to push the knot into the center hole in the spine board. If you start the sewing on the inside of the section, the tie-off will be in the center of the section.

Starting *inside* the section:

1. Exit the section and spine board at station 2.
2. Proceed to the head. Enter station 1 of the board and the section.
3. Proceed to the tail. Exit station 3 of the section and the board.
4. Enter station 2 of the board and the section. Entering the section, make sure the thread in step 5 is on the other side of the long stitch inside the section (step 3) than the starting thread (step 1).
   This is so when you tie-off, the knot will surround the long stitch attaching at station 2.
5. Tie-off with a square knot.

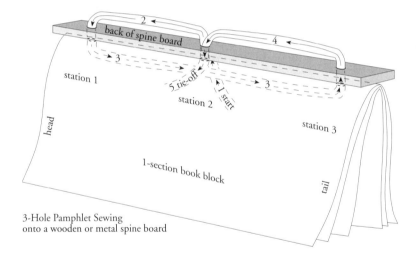

3-Hole Pamphlet Sewing
onto a wooden or metal spine board

The first sewing attaches the exposed-spine board to the section. Make sure the good side of the board faces the section. The illustration describes the sewing as starting inside the section for an exposed knot. If you wish to hide the tie-off, start the sewing at station 2 on the outside of the board and enter the board to the section as step 1.

Pamphlet sewing is a *B* stitch, not a figure *8*.

SECOND SEWING

The second sewing attaches the book block/spine board to the cover by stitching through the leather around the spine board. When the needle enters the leather to the inside it slips under the book block, over the spine board then exits the leather spine. I chose only to attach near the head and the tail, since I did not want stitches through the drawing on the spine. If you do not attach in the center of the spine, the spine board should be PVA glued to the leather. I did not and it seems secure.

Opening the cover reveals the exposed wooded spine board in the gutter. Opened to the back cover shows the ties-off of threads at the head and the tail. A thin strip of copper or brass as a spine board would add a nice texture.

Since this sample binding was rather extravagant, I imaged it as my Book Number 212.

The spine of this book is reproduced in color on the front cover of Volume V.

Acrobats, Book Number 212, Keith Smith, August 2002. Edition of 10. 18.5 x 14.5 x 1.5 cm.

SPAN & LINK

This 2-needle, 2-section sewing is elegant, but then I am writing this description immediately after sewing the first prototype which was designed as I sewed, so I have had no time to reflect.

The sewing consists of horizontal bars at the head and tail, where the threads span to the other section. The thread in the first section spans up to the second and the thread from the second section spans down to the first section. Since I sew this with the book standing on the tail, the spans are left to right and right to left.

Preparation

Make a 2-board cover reinforced with spine paper. In the example to the right I mistakenly added the spine paper after making the turn-ins, so it does not extend to the head and tail. In forming the stitches at station 9 and tying-off, I pulled tightly and puckered the leather at the tail. Had my spine paper been the full height of the cover this would not have happened.

SPAN & LINK: Tension determines the shape of the links. See illustrations on the following page.

The photo illustration on the previous page shows the links formed with a tight anchor stitch as shown in figure 1 below. The anchors alternate with each station allowing the larger link to be the darker color at every other station alternating with lighter links.

Even tension shows equal amounts of both threads for symmetry as in figure 2. The darker color is always on the left using either approach to tension in the sewing.

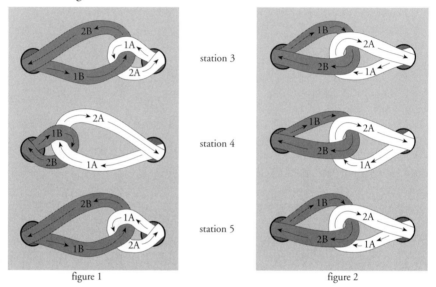

figure 1   figure 2

TENSION IN FORMING THE LINKS AT STATIONS 3–8:
On the left, forming the link with a tight anchor stitch gives an asymmetrical anchor/link
On the right, equal tension centers the link on the spine for equal amounts of both threads.

Sewing Stations

There are 8 sewing station on the spine in 2 rows with 9 sewing stations in the sections. Station 2 exists only in the sections as the means to start the sewing. Two colors of thread are tied together close to the ends of each. The excess beyond the knot is clipped so it appears to be one thread, half of which is one color and half another. A needle is placed on the end of each color.

Stations 1 and 9 of the cover are placed in the gutter. Stations 3–8 of the cover are placed closer together horizontally. Vertically, stations 3–8 are evenly spaced. This makes 8 stations for the spine-cover.

The section has 9 stations. Station 2 is for the sections, only and is positioned between stations 1 and 3. It is used to start the sewing by entering the sections, only, from the mountain peak to the valley. Pierce all the stations.

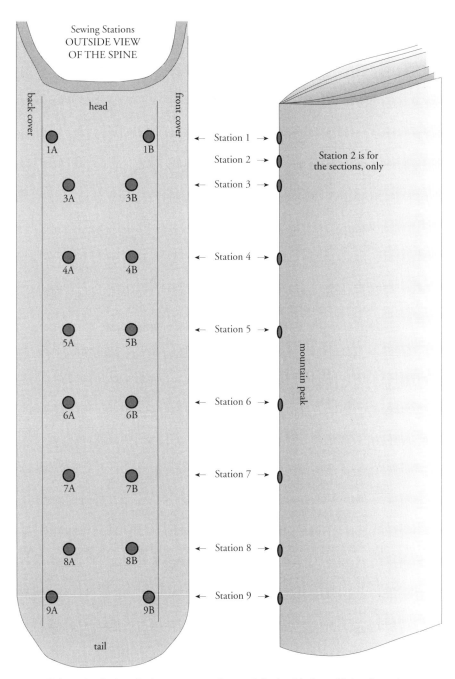

Sewing Stations
OUTSIDE VIEW
OF THE SPINE

back cover

head

front cover

1A   1B   ← Station 1 →

          Station 2 →   Station 2 is for
                              the sections, only

3A   3B   ← Station 3 →

4A   4B   ← Station 4 →

5A   5B   ← Station 5 →

mountain peak

6A   6B   ← Station 6 →

7A   7B   ← Station 7 →

8A   8B   ← Station 8 →

9A   9B   ← Station 9 →

tail

Eight sewing Stations for the cover are evenly spaced. Station 2 is then added to the sections.

PROCEDURE

1*a*. Set aside the cover. Take the needle with the darker color thread through the mountain peak of the first section at station 2. Pull the thread to the inside until the knot touches the section.

1*b*. Take the needle with the lighter color thread through the mountain peak of the second section at station 2. Pull the thread to the inside. Set on the cover.

2*a*. Proceed with the darker thread to station 1 in the first section. Exit station 1 of the first section and station 1*B* of the cover.

3*a*. The darker thread spans and enters station 1*A* of the cover and station 1 of the second section.

2*b*. Pick up the lighter color thread inside the second section. Proceed to and exit station 1 of the second section and 1*A* of the cover below and tangent to the horizontal darker thread on the spine.

3*b*. Span and enter station 1*B* of the cover and enter station 1 of the first section.

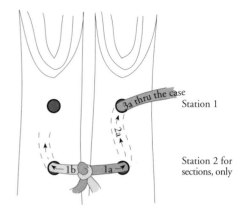

Station 1

Station 2 for sections, only

Start the sewing in the sections, only. Enter the mountain peaks of each section at station 2.

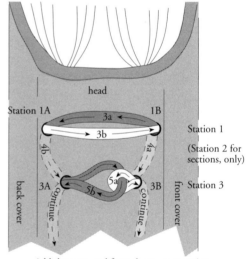

head

Station 1A

1B

Station 1

(Station 2 for sections, only)

Station 3

back cover

front cover

Add the cover and form the spans at station 1 with step 3.

4*a*. The lighter color thread exits station 3 of the first section and 3*B* of the cover.

5*a*. The lighter color thread re-enters 3*B* of the cover and station 3 of the first section. Pull most of the thread to the inside leaving a small loop on the spine. Do not pull all the thread to the inside or you will lose the loop and any sewing at this station.

For stations 3–8 the lighter color remains in the *B* stations of the first section.

4*b*. The darker color thread exits station 3 of the second section and 3*A* of the cover.

5*b*. The darker color thread links (goes through the loop of) the lighter color thread then re-enters 3*A* of the cover and station 3 of the second section. For stations 3–8 the darker color remains in the *B* stations of the second section.

Carefully adjust the tension of both threads to form the look of the link on the spine. You may wish equal amounts of color of the two threads as shown in figure 2 on page 164. Or, you may wish to keep the loop small and the link in a larger teardrop shape as in figure 1 in the same illustration.

Sewing the Remaining Link Stations

Sew stations 4–8 in a similar manner as the sewing at station 3. Linking alternates with the loop formed on alternating lettered stations on the spine.

Sewing the Final Span at the Tail

After completing the link at station 8 with step 15b, re-enter cover and section. Pick up the darker color thread inside the second section.

16a. Exit station 9 of the second section and 9*A* of the cover.

17a. Span and enter 9B of the cover and station 9 of the first section.

16b. Exit station 9 of the first section and 9*B* of the cover below the darker horizontal stitch.

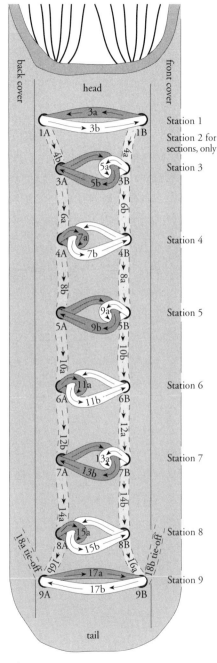

Sewing path of the Span & Link

17b. Span and enter 9*A* of the cover and station 9 of the second section. Make sure the 2 stitches on the spine do not overlap but are parallel.

18a. Tie-off the lighter color thread inside the second section with a half hitch at station 9. Clip the dangling thread so it does not hang out at the tail.

18b. Tie-off the darker color thread inside the first section with a half hitch at station 9. Clip the dangling thread.

The Span & Link is a 2-section sewing. 18.2 x 14.5 x 1.4 cm.

SPAN-SPAN

The double spans on the spine of this 2-section sewing look identical to the 1-section sewing called *Faux Double Raised Cords,* page 141.

The sewing pattern is taken from the traditional *Butterfly* sewing, described in *Exposed Spine Sewings,* Volume III Non-Adhesive Binding. The *Butterfly* is also known as *Japanese 4-Needle Sewing* or *Yamato Toji.* The *Butterfly* is limited structurally because it is an unsupported sewing.

The sewing described here, referred to as *Span-Span,* is a continuous support sewing since it is sewn through the leather spine. It is a 2-needle sewing.

PREPARATION

Prepare a 2-board cover, as described on page 61. Use spine paper. See page 76. You might wish to use end-cords, page 75. Prepare two sections.

Two colors of thread are tied together close to the ends of each. Excess beyond the knot is clipped. A needle is placed on the end of each color thread.

The 2-section *Span–Span* was designed because I liked the elegant look of the 1-section *Faux Double Raised Cords.* On the book shelf you cannot tell them apart. Of course they have very different sewing paths. 18.2 x 14.5 x 1.4 cm. This binding is reproduced on the cover.

Inside view of the center of each section of the *Span-Span* reveals the stitches. They alternate light and dark in the first section and dark and light in the second, pictured above.

Inside of the 2-board cover is shown above reinforced with spine paper. End cords were placed at the head and tail prior to making the leather turn-ins. A different color kangaroo leather was inlaid between the turn-ins and the inside leather, which is a third color. Pencil lines were drawn on the inside papers after they were attached to the boards.

Below is the outside of the cover.

Sewing Stations

There can be any number of even- or odd-numbered stations. The description will use 7 stations pierced in the book block. Since Stations 1 and 7 are used inside the cover to start and to finish the sewing, they are not pierced in the cover. The cover pierces stations 2, 3, 4, 5 and 6 where double stitches will span the spine.

Design the spine so that the five double spans are equally positioned on the spine. Leave a little more space between station 6 and the tail than from station 2 and the head. This will give a little more of a base to the closed book on the shelf.

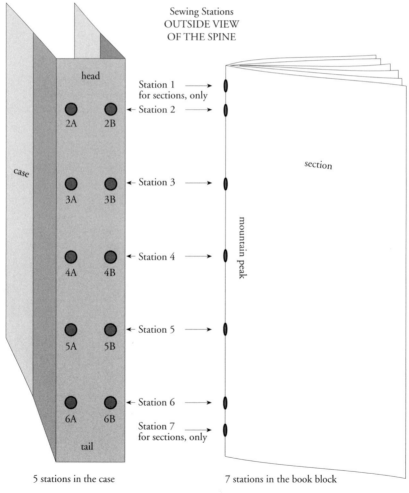

In planning the stations for the cover make sure there is room for stations 1 and 7 in the sections, which are not as tall as the cover.

The sewing is started in the mountain peaks of the sections similar to the Span & Link, but starting in station 1 instead of 2.

The *A* stations are the second section. The *B*s are the first. Colors of thread alternate inside the sections. On the spine the lighter color is always the horizontal stitch (span) on top of, and tangent to, the darker color. The lighter color thread always exits first to form the span before the darker color exits.

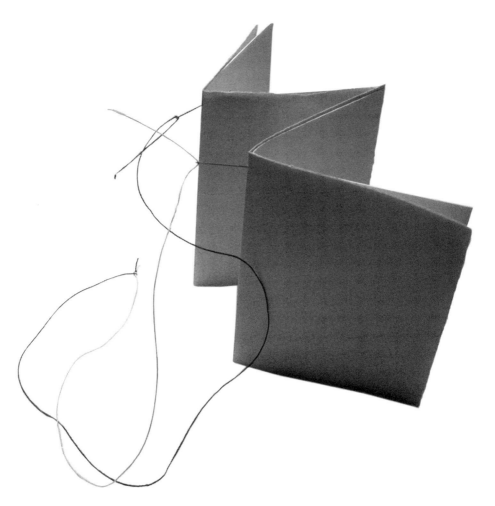

Set aside the cover. Start the sewing from the mountain peak to the valley at station 1. The lighter color thread enters the first section. The darker color starts in the second section.

SEWING PROCEDURE

1*a*. Set aside the cover. Take the needle with the lighter color thread through the mountain peak of the first section at station 1. Pull the thread to the inside until the knot touches the section.

1*b*. Take the needle with the darker color thread through the mountain peak of the second section at station 1. Pull the thread to the inside. Set on the cover.

2*a*. Pick up the lighter color thread inside the first section. Proceed to and exit station 2 of the section and 2*B* of the cover.

3*a*. The lighter thread *spans* and enters station 2*A* of the cover and 2 of the second section.

2*b*. Proceed with the darker color thread to station 2 in the second section. Exit station 2 of the section and station 2*A* of the cover below and tangent to the horizontal lighter thread on the spine.

3*b*. Span and enter station 2*B* of the cover and enter station 2 of the first section.

4*a*. Proceed inside the second section with the lighter color thread to station 3. Exit station 3 of the section and station 3*A* of the cover.

5*a*. Span and enter station 3*B* of the cover and station 3 of the first section with the lighter color thread.

4*b*. Proceed inside the first section with the darker color thread to station 3. Exit station 3 of the section and station 3*B* of the cover.

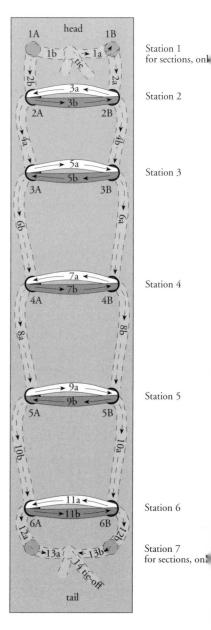

OUTSIDE VIEW OF THE SPINE: Sewing path of the 2-section *Span-Span* uses 2 needles.

5*b*. Span and enter station 3*A* of the cover and station 3 of the second section with the darker color thread.

6*a*. Proceed inside the first section with the lighter color thread to station 4. Exit station 4 of the section and station 4*B* of the cover .

7*a*. Span and enter station 4*A* of the cover and station 4 of the second section with the lighter color thread.

6*b*. Proceed inside the second section with the darker color thread to station 4. Exit station 4 of the section and station 4*A* of the cover.

7*b*. Span and enter station 4*B* of the cover and station 4 of the first section with the darker color thread.

Repeat the sewing pattern of steps 4–7 at stations 5 and 6:

8*a*. Proceed inside the second section with the lighter color thread to station 5. Exit station 5 of the section and station 5*A* of the cover.

9*a*. Span and enter station 5*B* of the cover and station 5 of the first section.

8*b*. Proceed inside the first section with the darker color thread to station 5. Exit station 5 of the section and 5*B* of the cover.

9*b*. Span and enter station 5*A* of the cover and station 5 of the second section with the darker color thread.

10*a*.Proceed inside the first section with the lighter color thread to station 6. Exit station 6 of the section and station 6*B* of the cover .

11*a*.Span and enter station 6*A* of the cover and station 6 of the second section with the lighter color thread.

10*b*. Proceed inside the second section with the darker color thread to station 6. Exit station 6 of the section and station 6*A* of the cover.

11*b*. Span and enter station 6*B* of the cover and station 6 of the first section with the darker color thread.

Finishing the Sewing

12*a*.Proceed inside the second section with the lighter color. Exit station 7 of the section. Do not exit the cover as there is no station 7 for the cover.

12*b*. Proceed inside the first section with the darker color. Exit station 7 of the section.

13*a,b*. Pull the two threads together and tie a square knot between the sections against the inside of the cover. Clip the dangling threads short.

X SEWING

Several sewings were created for Volume II, *1-, 2- & 3-Section Sewings* which I titled *Twisted* X, or some variation thereof. Any sewings from that book can be adapted for these hard cover leather bindings.

The quarter leather on the outside of the cover is inlaid in 3 colors using 5 pieces of leather. It is described at length beginning on page 181.

PREPARATION

Prepare a 2-board cover, as described on page 61. Use spine paper, page 76. You might wish to use end-cords, page 75. Prepare two sections.

This is a 2-needle sewing using one color of thread. A needle is placed on each end of the thread.

Several variations for the sewing are described on page 184.

The *X* Sewing uses 2 needles, one one each end of a single thread. The quarter leather spine is inlaid in 3 colors of leather in horizontal strips. Inlaying is described on page 181.
The inlays of leather on the spine can be seen in color on the front cover of Volume V.

Sewing Stations

NUMBER OF Xs: Each X on the spine requires two sets of stations.

The description shows 5 *Xs*, which requires 10 stations. With the span at the head, only, total number of stations will be 11.

The cover and each section pierce all the stations.

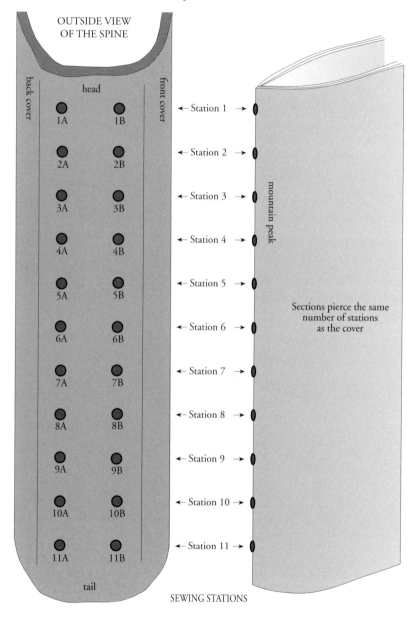

OUTSIDE VIEW
OF THE SPINE

back cover

head

front cover

← Station 1 →
1A   1B

← Station 2 →
2A   2B

← Station 3 →
3A   3B

← Station 4 →
4A   4B

← Station 5 →
5A   5B

← Station 6 →
6A   6B

← Station 7 →
7A   7B

← Station 8 →
8A   8B

← Station 9 →
9A   9B

← Station 10 →
10A   10B

← Station 11 →
11A   11B

tail

mountain peak

Sections pierce the same
number of stations
as the cover

SEWING STATIONS

INLAID LEATHER ON THE OUTSIDE OF THE COVER

Since the last several covers have inlaid leather between the seams of the turn-ins and the inside leather, I thought I would try that on the outside of the cover. The following pages show the progression for inlaying leather for the outside of the cover.

Pencil lines were drawn on the outside of the boards as a guide. I started with the middle piece of leather which was a scrap and far wider than needed. It will be trimmed to proper width later. Two thin horizontal strips of very dark leather were added above and below. The pieces to be turned-in were added last.

SPINE PAPER IS NECESSARY: If the spine is strips of inlaid leather, a one-piece hinge connects the various strips on the spine. If the hinge is inlaid strips of leather, it is critical to include the vertical spine paper which connects all the horizontal strips of leather. Use Tyvek as the spine paper for strength. See: *spine paper,* page 76.

Inlaying leather for the outside of the board. Draw your shapes on the board with pencil. Start in the middle and work out to the head and tail.

ABOVE: Add the spine paper and end cords. Make the turn-ins to the inside of the boards.If strips of leather are inlaid on both the spine and hinge, the spine paper is important as it connects the various pieces of leather.

BELOW: Trim the leather on the outside of the boards. Compare this horizontal pattern of inlaid quarter leather to the vertical inlays on page 204.

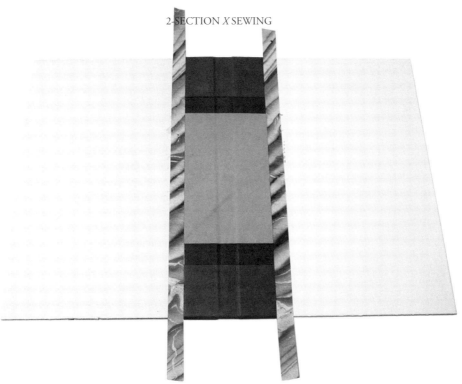

After the leathers are trimmed on the front of the board the remainder of the boards are covered with decorative papers. Start by butting the papers which are tangent to the leather. Add the next papers which are butted to that paper. Keep adding any remaining papers which extend beyond the foredge. Make the turn-ins. Always work from the inside out.

VARIATIONS FOR THIS SEWING

ELIMINATING THE SPAN AT THE HEAD: To have only *X*s on the spine, do not piece station 1 in the cover. Start the sewing in the mountain peaks of the sections as in the previous sewing. if you choose to do this, the *X*s on the spine should be repositioned slightly closer toward the head.

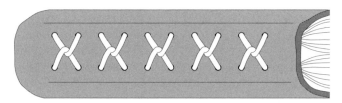

Eliminating the span at the head shows only *X*s on the spine.

ADDING A SPAN AT THE TAIL: If you wish the sewn design on the spine to be symmetrical, add a span at the tail reflecting the span at station 1. This second span is not described. You would add a station after the final *X*.

Instead of tying-off inside each section, one thread will exit the final station of either section and the cover. It spans and enters the paired station on the cover into the other section. Tie-off the two threads with a square knot.

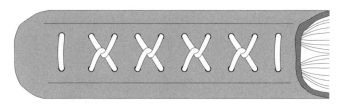

Adding a span at the tail gives symmetry.

TYPE OF X: The pattern on the spine can be varied by angling to form a straight diagonal *X*, by linking to form a linked *X* or by twisting the thread to form a twisted *X*.

1. straight *X* 2. linked *X* 3. twisted *X*

Choose which type of *X* you wish to form.

184

Sewing with 2 Colors of Thread

You can sew with two colors of thread if you eliminate the span at the head as illustrated at the top of the facing page. Start the sewing as with the *Span-Span,* page 171. Tie together the two colors of thread and enter the sections from the mountain peak.

• The straight *X* will alternate the color from section to section.
• The linked *X* will always have the same color thread in each section.
• The twisted *X* will alternate the color from section to section.

 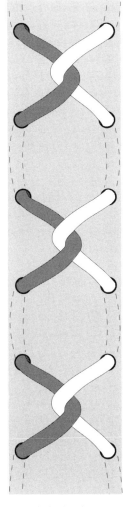 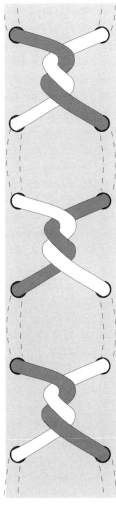

The straight *X* alternates color in the sections.

The linked *X* has the same color in each section.

The twisted *X* alternates color in the sections.

SEWING PROCEDURE

1a. Start on the outside of the cover. Take one needle through station 1*A* of the cover and station 1 of the second section. Pull half the thread to the inside.

1b. Take the other needle through station 1*B* of the cover and station 1 of the first section.

2a. Exit station 2 of the first section and 2*B* of the cover.

2b. Exit station 2 of the second section and 2*A* of the cover.

3a, b. *FOR A STRAIGHT* X:

Take the thread extending from station 2*A* and enter station 3*B* of the cover and 3 of the first section. The thread extending from station 2*B* *angles* (drops at a diagonal) and enters station 3*A* of the cover and 3 of the second section.

FOR A LINKED X:

Take the thread extending from station 2*A* and enter station 3*A* of the cover and 3 of the second section. The thread extending from 2*B* angles and links the other thread before entering station 3*B* of the cover and 3 of the first section. Adjust the tension of the two threads to form an *X*.

FOR A TWISTED X:

Twist the threads. One thread will enter either station 3*A* or 3*B* of the cover into the section. The other thread enters the remaining third station.

4a. Proceed inside the first section to the next station. Exit.

4b. Proceed inside the second section to the next station. Exit.

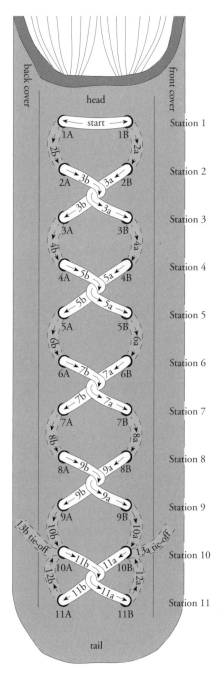

Sewing pattern for the *X* Sewing.

Sewing the Remaining Stations:

Repeat steps 3 and 4 to form each additional *X*.

Tying-Off:

After forming the final X each thread enters the cover and a section. Proceed back to the previous station. Tie-off with a half hitch. Each section is tied-off separately.

Completed 2-section *X* Sewing with inlaid kangaroo leathers on the spine.

TWISTED LONG STITCH

There is something nice about sewing with double threads, especially when they are two different colors. This sewing starts out with a single thread in one color. A second color thread is introduced and twisted into a 2-ply stitch as in a candy cane or barber pole.

PREPARATION

Prepare a 2-board cover, as described on page 61. Use spine paper, page 76. The spine paper should be as stiff as Canson or Stonehenge paper because you will be stitching around the head and the tail.

Threads

This is a 6-needle sewing requiring 3 threads with a needle on each end. Two threads of the same color are used to sew each section separately to the cover. These threads should be about 13/4 times the height of the cover. The third thread is of contrasting color used to form the twist. It should be approximately 21/2 times the height of the cover.

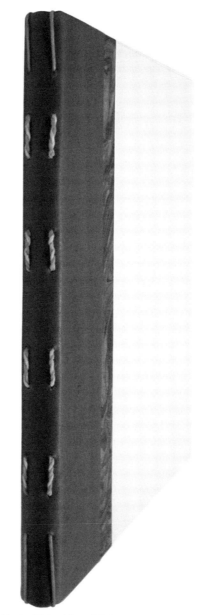

2–Section Twisted Long Stitch

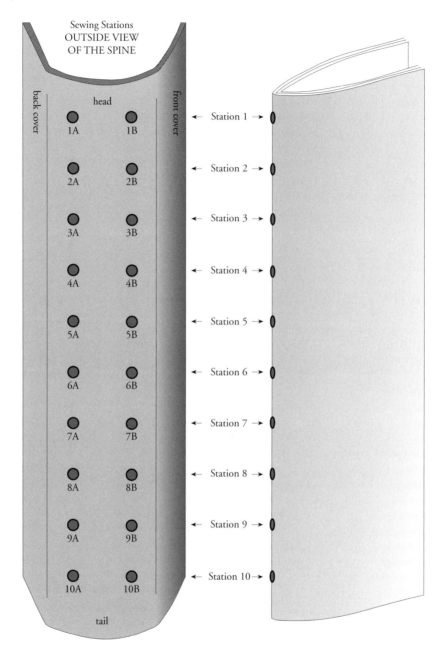

The cover has 2 rows of 10 equally spaced stations. The sections have 10 stations which align with the cover stations. The first section is sewn down the *B* stations. A separate sewing down the *A* station attaches the second section.

Sewing Stations

There are 10 stations on the spine of the cover and the same number aligned on the sections. Station 1 and 10 go around the head and tail. The remaining stations form 4 long stitches on the spine.

If you wish longer stitches, change from 8 stations for 4 long stitches to only 6 stations to create 3 long stitches, plus 2 stations to go around the head and tail.

SEWING PROCEDURE

Set aside the book block. The longer thread used to form the twist exits the cover, only, at station 2. Take one needle to the outside at station 2*A* and the other needle out station 2*B*. Center the threads on the spine.

To start the sewing, add the light color of thread to the cover, only. Exit station 2*A* and 2*B*.

At step 5 in sewing the first section, you might want to take the thread extending from station 2*A* up over the head and keep it temporarily inside between the section and the back cover. Otherwise it tends to get in the way in forming the twists with the two threads extending from station 2*B*.

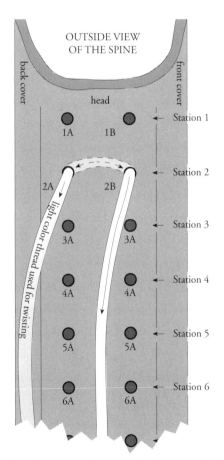

The third thread, shown as the lighter color is used to form the twist with the two darker sewings. Exit station 2*A* and 2*B* of the cover, only with the longest thread.

191

Set on the first section to be sewn. One of the shorter, darker color threads is used. This first sewing will be down the *B* stations.

1. Start on the inside of the section. Exit station 1 of the section and 1*B* of the cover. Pull all but about 6″ of thread to the outside.

   Proceed to the head. Go around the head to the inside of the middle of the section.

2. Proceed to station 1.

3. Tie a square knot and clip the shorter thread near the knot.

4. Proceed on the inside to station 2. Exit station 2 of the section and 2*B* of the cover. Be sure not to pierce the other thread which extends from this station.

5. Grasp both threads protruding from station 2*B*. Twist them a few or several times to form the desired number of twists between station 2*B* and 3*B*. Enter station 3*B* of the cover and station 3 of the section with each thread one at a time. Check the look of the twisted long stitch.

6. Proceed to station 4. Threads can be twisted on the inside of the section or left parallel. Exit station 4 of the section and 4*B* of the cover with each thread individually.

7. Grasp both threads protruding from station 4*B*. Twist them between station 4*B* and 5*B*. Enter station 5*B* of the cover and station 5 of the section, with each thread separately.

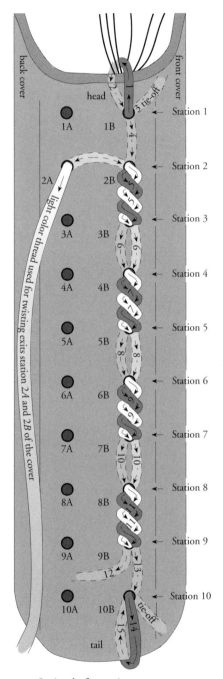

Sewing the first section.

192

8. Proceed to station 6. Exit station 6 of the section and 6B of the cover with each thread individually.

9. Twist both threads protruding from station 6B between station 6B and 7B. Enter station 7B of the cover and station 7 of the section, with each thread separately.

10. Proceed to station 8. Exit station 8 and 8B with each thread separately.

11. Twist both threads protruding from station 8B between station 8B and 9B. Enter station 9B of the cover and 9 of the section, with only the color thread that extends around the head.

12. Take the other thread which has been twisted and enter the cover, only. This will be tied off after sewing the second section.

13. Open the section. With the thread inside the section, proceed to station 10 and exit the section and 10B of the cover.

14. Proceed on the outside of the spine to the tail. Wrap around the tail to the inside of the section.

15. Proceed inside the section to station 10. Tie-off with a half hitch.

Sewing the Second Section

Use the remaining thread which is the same color used to sew the first. Sew the second section down the A stations of the cover in the same manner as steps 1–15 used to sew the first section, with this difference in step 12.

12. At station 9 take the thread remaining on the spine and enter the cover, only. Tie-off between the sections with the same color thread from the first section.

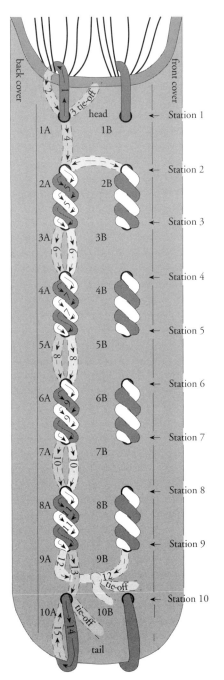

Sewing the second section.

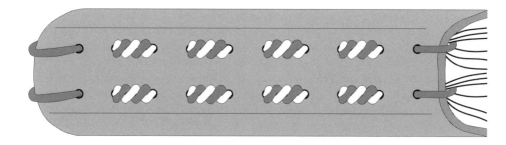

Drawing of the 2-Section Twisted Long Stitch.

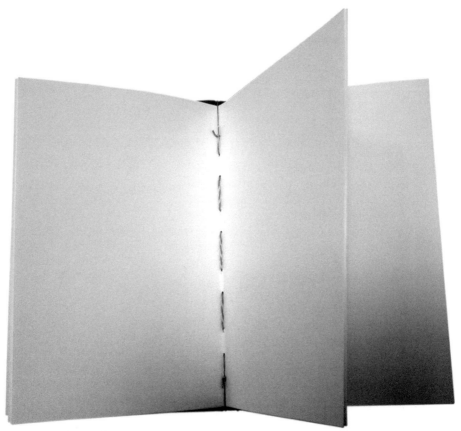

The two color threads on the inside can be twisted as above, or parallel, as in the diagram on the previous page. Each thread enters and exits separately.

2-Section Twisted Long Stitch shown here with kangaroo quarter leather and a decorative paper called Florentine Fruit. 18.5 x 14.5 x 1.8 cm.

The turn-ins at the foredge are large. To show more of the Florentine paper, the inside laid papers were cut at irregular angles. The 2-thread stitches inside the sections are twisted.

TWISTED SPAN

After designing the previous sewing the obvious next attempt would be two color threads twisted as horizontal rather than vertical stitches.

Actually, it is impossible to twist the two threads when they exit to the spine as they are headed in opposite directions. One thread spans and enters the cover and the other section. I chose the lighter color for this. The darker color spans by means of a series of loops using the lighter color thread as a support. Since the lighter color starts inside the first section, which is the *B* stations on the spine, it spans right to left at station 1. It then drops and exits an *A* station and spans left to right, alternating the direction of the span-as-support. The thread that loops to form the span will alternate directions as well. Thus the pattern of the spiralling loops slants to the right then to the left.

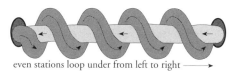

even stations loop under from left to right ⟶

⟵ odd stations loop under from right to left

The series of loops forming the spiralling span alternate the direction of the slant.

PREPARATION

Prepare a 2-board cover, as described on page 61. Use spine paper as described on page 76.

Threads

This is a 2-needle sewing. Two threads of contrasting color are tied together with a needle on each end.

Sewing Stations

The spine-cover has 2 rows of 8 equally spaced stations, labeled as station 1 and stations 3–9. The sections have one additional station to start the sewing. This is labeled as station 2. *Do not* pierce station 2 in the cover.

SEWING PROCEDURE

The sewing starts in the same manner as the Span & Link, page 163, and as described below. Look at the illustration on page 166. The only difference is in this sewing the lighter color thread enters the first section and the darker enters the second.

1a. Set aside the cover. Take the needle with the lighter color thread through the mountain peak of the first section at station 2. Pull the thread to the inside until the knot touches the section.

1b. Take the needle with the darker color thread through the mountain peak of the second section at station 2. Pull the thread to the inside. Set on the cover.

2a. Proceed with the lighter thread to station 1 in the first section. Exit station 1 of the first section and station 1*B* of the cover.

3a. The lighter thread *spans* and enters station 1*A* of the cover and station 1 of the second section.

2b. Pick up the darker color thread inside the second section. Proceed to and exit station 1 of the second section and 1*A* of the cover below and tangent to the horizontal darker thread on the spine. Do not pierce the lighter color thread.

3b. Form a series of equally spaced loops, approximately 4, as illustrated on the previous page. The needle always slips *under* the lighter thread support. Be careful not to scar the leather. Enter station 1*A* of the cover and station 1 of the first section.

4a. The lighter color thread exits the next station (2) of the second section and station *B* of the cover.

5a. The lighter color thread spans and enters the same numbered *A* station of the cover and station the first section.

4b. The darker color thread exits the next station (2) of the first section and *A* station of the cover.

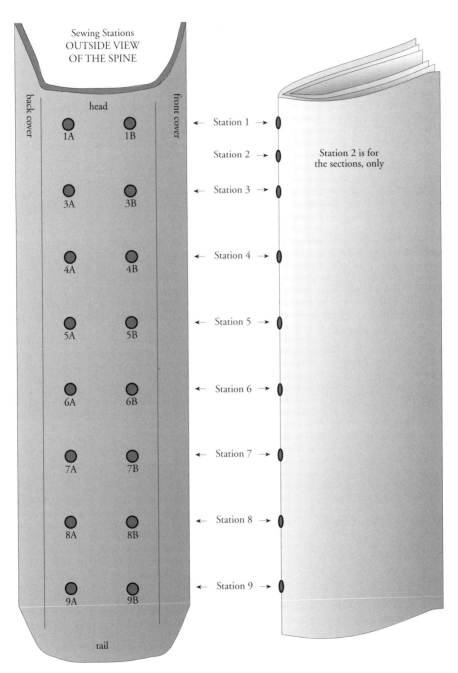

Sewing Stations
OUTSIDE VIEW
OF THE SPINE

back cover

head

front cover

1A 1B ← Station 1 →

Station 2 → Station 2 is for
the sections, only

3A 3B ← Station 3 →

4A 4B ← Station 4 →

5A 5B ← Station 5 →

6A 6B ← Station 6 →

7A 7B ← Station 7 →

8A 8B ← Station 8 →

9A 9B ← Station 9 →

tail

The cover has 2 rows of 9 equally spaced stations. Station 2 is not pierced in the cover.
Station 2 is in the sections, only. Sewing starts through the mountain peaks of station 2.

5b. Form the same number of equally spaced loops as before, slipping under the lighter thread support. Enter the same numbered *B* station of the cover and station the second section.

6a. The lighter color thread exits the next station (3) of the first section and station *A* of the cover.

7a. The lighter color thread spans and enters the same numbered *B* station of the cover and station the second section.

6b. The darker color thread exits the next station (3) of the second section and *B* station of the cover.

7b. Form the same number of equally spaced loops as before, slipping under the lighter thread support. Enter the same numbered *A* station of the cover and station the first section.

Sewing the Remaining Even-Numbered Stations

Repeat steps 4a, b–5a, b.

Sewing the Remaining Odd-Numbered Stations

Repeat steps 6a, b–7a, b.

Tying-Off

After the lighter color thread enters station 10*A* of the cover and 10 of the first section, tie-off with a half hitch.

After the darker color thread loops and enters station 10*B* of the cover and 10 of the second section, tie-off with a half hitch.

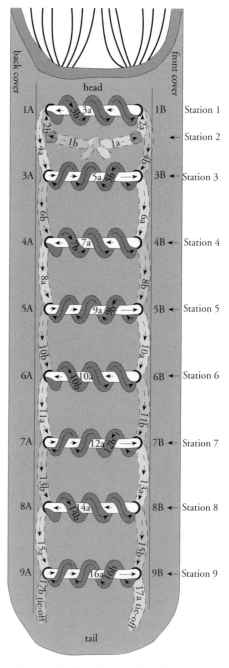

Sewing path of the 2-Section Twisted Span.

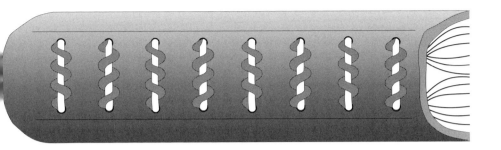

In a good design the pattern of the sewing on the inside of the book is pleasing as well as the sewing on the spine. Here, a single thread is seen from station to station. Each stitch alternates from the lighter to the darker color thread.

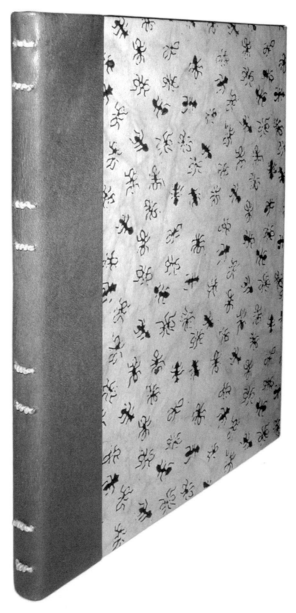

A dark color quarter leather was applied to the boards. Then a lighter, vertical strip of leather was placed on the front board tangent to the darker leather. The same was done with the back cover. The remainder of the boards was covered with a laid paper.

Compare this vertical inlay of leather to a horizontal inlay described on pages 181–183.

The sewing above is reproduced in color on the back cover of Volume V.

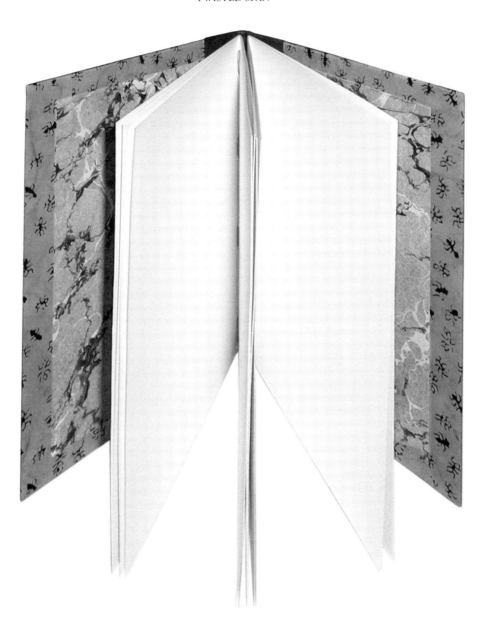

Above and on the facing page are two views of the same 2-Section Twisted Span. Decorative papers were added to the boards after sewing.

6 SPANS

This 2-needle, 2-section sewing is anti-climactic. After spending so much time making the cover, I think I was afraid to attempt a more elaborate sewing.

Before I am draw in a blank hand-bound book, I tend to sew several before I begin. If I mess up one book, I start on the next.

One has to be willing to fail. I was timid, not up to the task of devising a better sewing.

This sewing has 6 horizontal bars at the head and tail. One needle spans from the first section to the second then drops down 2 stations to exit and span. The other needle spans from the second to the first section then drops to exit and span.

Preparation

Prepare a 2-board cover, as described on page 61. Use spine paper. See page 76. You might wish to use end cords, page 75. Prepare two sections.

This is a 2-needle sewing using one color of thread. A needle is placed on each end of the thread.

Sewing Stations

There are 6 pairs of stations which requires 12 holes on the cover.Sections pierce all 6 stations.

SEWING PROCEDURE

Start the sewing on the outside of the spine. The first needle to be used will be referred to as the *a* needle. The other needle will be the *b* needle.

1*a*. Take the *a* needle through station 1*A* of the cover into station 1 of the second section, which is on the left when viewing the outside of the spine.

1*b*. Take the remaining (*b*) needle through station 1*B* of the cover into station 1 of the first section.

2*a*. Proceed to station 2 inside the second section with the *a* needle. Exit station 2 and 2*A* of the cover.

2*b*. Proceed to station 3 inside the first section with the *b* needle. Exit station 3 and 3*B* of the cover.

3*a*. With the *a* needle, span to station 2*B*. Enter station 2*B* of the cover and station 2 of the first section.

3*b*. With the *b* needle, span to station 3*A*. Enter station 3*A* of the cover and station 3 of the second section.

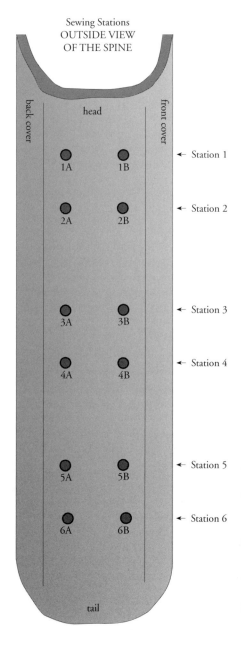

Sewing stations for 6 Spans

4a. With the *a* needle, proceed to station 4 inside the first section. Exit station 4 and 4*B* of the cover.

4b. With the *b* needle, proceed to station 5 inside the second section. Exit station 5 and 5*A* of the cover.

5a. With the *a* needle, span to station 4*A*. Enter station 4*A* of the cover and 4 of the second section.

5b. With the *b* needle, span to station 5*B*. Enter station 5*B* of the cover and station 5 of the first section.

6a. With the *a* needle, proceed to station 6 inside the second section. Exit station 6 and 6*A* of the cover.

7a. With the *a* needle, span to station 6*B*. Enter station 6*B* of the cover and station 6 of the first section.

Tying-Off

Tie-off the two threads diagrammed as 8*a* and 6*b* inside the first section with a square knot.

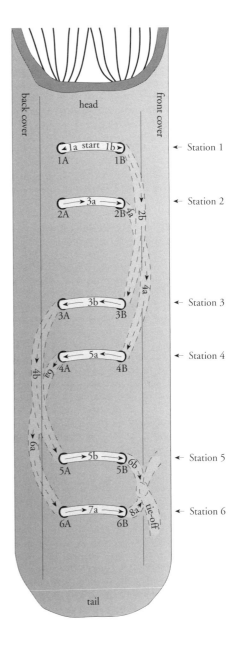

Sewing path for 6 Spans

DARTING PACKED STITCH

Each of the 3 sections is sewn separately with a different color thread. The head and tail have variable size stitches that go around the end to the inside of the sections. The middle section is sewn first with a vertical running stitch.

One of the end sections is sewn next, coming out on the spine at a diagonal to pack every other stitch of the second sewing. The remaining section is sewn in the same manner. The sewing reminds me of flying insects darting this way and that.

PREPARATION

Make your cover and cut three sections to fit. I suggest rather thick sections for this binding, so the diagonal stitches on the spine will have some length.

Sewing Stations

The first and last numbered stations are on a diagonal:

Station 1 at the head is a different length for each section so the ends of the resulting stitches form a diagonal. The diagonal is down from the head on the left of the spine and closer on the right.

At the tail, the final station, 14, is close to the tail on the left of the spine and up from the tail on the right.

Darting Packed Stitch is a 3-section sewing.

Stations 2–13 are based on a right angle grid. In designing the stations on the template, the intersections on the grid will show stations 2–13 as twelve rows, three abreast. Circle or mark the stencil for only the stations which will be pierced. In the diagram to the right, the white circles represent stations which will *not* be pierced.

Looking at the spine from the outside, the first vertical row of stations is lettered *A* and sews on the third section. The middle row is lettered *B* and sews the second section. The third row, far right, is lettered *C* and sews on the first (opening) section of the book.

For the A stations (last section in the book) pierce stations 1, 6, 7, 12, 13 and 14 in the section and the cover.

For the *B* stations, the middle section, pierce stations 1, 2, 3, 5, 6, 8, 9, 11, 12 and 14 in the section and the cover.

For the C stations (first section in the book) pierce stations 1, 3, 4, 9, 10 and 14 in the section and the cover.

Do *not* pierce the white circles in the diagram. These appear only in the pattern when determining the rows of sewing stations.

Sewing stations. Mark and pierce only the holes that are dark. The white circles only show the grid structure.

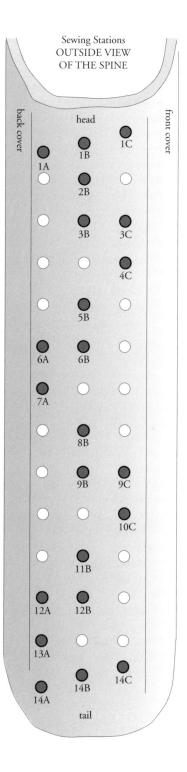

Sewing Stations
OUTSIDE VIEW
OF THE SPINE

back cover

front cover

head

tail

SEWING PROCEDURE

The center section is sewn first as described in the steps below. After wrapping around the head, the thread proceeds inside the section to station1. The knot is tied exactly at station 1. Then the sewing proceeds in and out the stations, towards the tail, in what is referred to as a *running stitch*.

This creates long stitches on the spine. These are needed in order to sew the other two sections which will pack these long stitches.

Sewing the Middle Section

The middle color (value) thread is used to sew the middle section.

1. Set on the second (middle) section. Exit station 1 of the section and out station 1*B* of the cover. Proceed to the head and wrap around to the inside of the section. Proceed to station 1.

2. Tie-off with a square knot exactly at station 1. Clip the shorter thread to 1/2″.

3. Proceed on the inside to station 2. Exit the section at station 2 and cover at 2*B*.

4. Proceed on the spine. Enter 3*B* of the cover and station 3 of the section.

5. Proceed on the inside to station 5. Exit the section at station 5 and cover at 5*B*.

6. Proceed on the spine. Enter 6*B* of the cover and station 6 of the section.

STARTING THE SEWING: The middle section is sewn first with a middle value (color) thread.

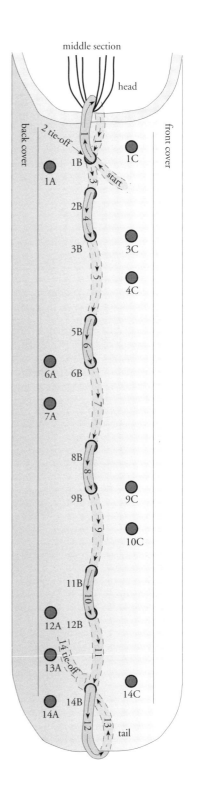

Sewing the Remaining Stations of the Middle Section

7.–10. Continue sewing in this manner, with the running stitch, until you enter station 12*B* of the cover and station 12 of the section with step 10. Step 11 will add the vertical stitch at the tail:

11. Proceed inside the section to station 14. Exit 14 of the section and station 14*B* of the cover.

12. Proceed on the spine towards the tail. Wrap around the tail to the inside of the section.

13. Proceed inside the section to station 14.

14. Tie-off with a half hitch at station 14. Clip the thread to 1/2″. Each section is sewn with a separate thread.

MIDDLE AND FIRST SECTIONS SEWN: As in the diagram on the facing page, the middle and first sections have been sewn. The third and final section will now be added and sewn, packing the two remaining long stitches of the middle section.

Views of the spine with all three sections sewn are on pages 211 and 216.

Sewing the Next Section

The next section to be sewn will be the first section in the book which will be sewn down the *C* stations of the cover. The lightest color thread is used to sew this section.

1. Set on the first section of the book block. Exit station 1 of the section and station 1*C* of the cover. Proceed to the head. Wrap around to the inside of the section. Proceed to station 1.

2. Tie-off with a square knot at station 1. Clip the shorter thread to 1/2″.

3. Proceed on the inside to station 3. Exit the section at station 3 and cover at 3*C*.

4. Climb at a diagonal, that is, *angle* to station 2*B*. Pass over the long stitch, that is, *lap* the stitch. *Loop* the stitch, that is, encircle it, as many times as you can. This is referred to as *packing*. A solid pack completely covers the long stitch with coils of thread. In the illustrations there are 4 loops. Number of loops depends upon the length of your long stitches and the thickness of thread. Keep the loops uniform in size. They will probably be more diagonal than horizontal. After you have packed the long stitch between stations 2*B* and 3*B*, angle and enter 4*C* of the cover and station 4 of section 1.

5. Proceed on the inside to station 9. Exit the section at station 9 and cover at 9*C*.

STARTING THE NEXT SEWING: The first section of the book is sewn next.

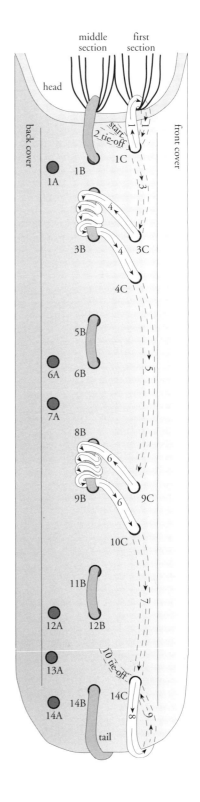

6. Angle towards station 8*B*. Lap the long stitch.
   Loop as many times as necessary to form a solid pack. If the long stitch between 8*B* and 9*B* is the same length as the previous, loop the same number of times as before.
   Angle and enter 10*C* of the cover and station 10 of section 1.
7. Proceed on the inside to station 14. Exit the section at station 14 and cover at 14*C*.
10. Proceed on the outside towards the tail. Wrap around the tail to the inside of the section.
11. Proceed inside the section to station 14.
12. Tie-off with a half hitch at station 14. Clip the thread to 1/2″.

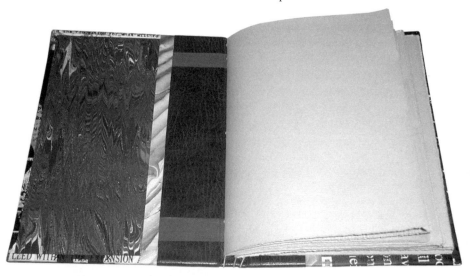

Above: Opened front cover of this binding shows a leather hinge of dark brown calf with inlaid strips of burgundy kangaroo.
Below: This example of the Darting Packed Stitch has 17 sewing stations with 5 rather than 4 packed stitches. It has a better proportion.

Sewing the Last Section

The third section to be sewn will be the final section in the book and will be sewn down the *A* stations of the cover. A darker color thread is used to sew this section.

1. Set on the last section. Exit station 1 of the section and station 1*A* of the cover. Proceed to the head. Wrap around to the inside of the section. Proceed to station 1.

2. Tie-off with a square knot at station 1. Clip the shorter thread to 1/2″.

3. Proceed on the inside to station 6. Exit the section at station 6 and cover at 6*A*.

4. Angle to station 5*B*. Lap the long stitch.
   Loop as many times as necessary to form a solid pack.
   Angle and enter 7*A* of the cover and station 7 of third section.

5. Proceed on the inside to station 12. Exit the section at station 12 and cover at 12*A*.

6. Angle towards station 11*B*. Lap the long stitch.
   Lap the long stitch.
   Loop as many times as necessary to form a solid pack.
   Angle and enter 13*A* of the cover and station 13 of third section.

7. Proceed on the inside to station 17. Exit the section at station 17 and cover at 17*A*.

8. Proceed on the outside towards the tail. Wrap around the tail to the inside of the section.

9. Proceed inside the section to station 17.

10. Tie-off with a half hitch at station 17. Clip the thread to 1/2″.

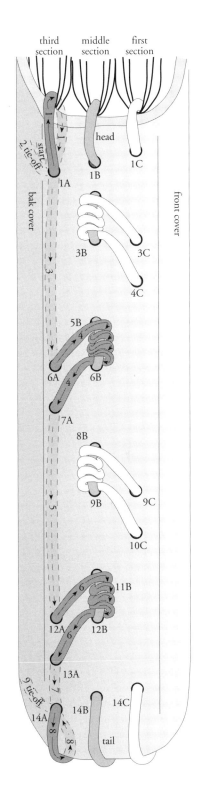

BRAIDED HANDLE BOOK I

A book with its own handle came to mind. There is the traditional girdle book. Monks wore a book of their daily prayers on their habit. Mine was something more akin to carrying a lunch bucket.

Who would carry such a book? I don't know. Someone might have a use for it. Then I thought, I have not gotten Bella anything for her second birthday. Why not make her a little sketch book she can carry around. She might even draw in the book! But, if not, she might like to carry—or more likely, throw the book. The handle might come in handy.

I designed three books with braided handles. I will show them in order. The final book, page 233, became Bella's book.

All the handle books have two sewings. The first sewing attaches the book block at the center of the spine. The second sewing adds the handle attached to the book block and the spine of the cover at the head and the tail.

PREPARATION

Prepare a 2-board cover, as described on page 61. Use spine paper, page 76. The spine paper should be a thick paper since you will be stitching around the head and the tail.

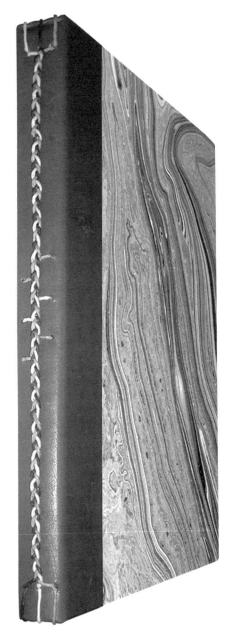

Braided Handle Book No. 1 has a taut handle which will stretch slightly with use.

Threads for the First Sewing

The first sewing uses two colors of thread tied together at one end so it appears to be one length of thread with a knot in the middle. Clip the shorter ends of thread close to the knot. Smash the knot so it does not bulge. I suggest you use a weaver's knot instead of a square knot as it has less bulk.

Place a needle on each end as this is a 2-needle sewing. This thread should be about 4 times the height of the cover.

Threads for the Second Sewing

The second sewing requires *three* separate threads each with one needle. Length of each thread should be about four times the height of the cover.

Designing the Stations

There are 8 sewing stations with 3 rows of stations on the spine. However, not all of the stations are pierced on the spine or in the sections. The diagram shows which stations to pre-pierce on the spine of the cover. The white circles *are not* pierced. They appear only to set up the grid before choosing which stations to pierce.

Do *not* pierce the white circles in the diagram.
COVER STATIONS: The cover pierces stations 1*A*, *B* and *C*; stations 2*B* and *C*; 3*A* and B; 4*B* and *C*; 5*A* and *B*; 6*B* and *C*; 7*A* and B; 8*A*, *B* and *C*.
BOOK BLOCK STATIONS: The first section pierces stations 1, 2, 4, 6 and 8. The second section pierces all 8 stations. The third section pierces stations 1, 3, 5, 7 and 8.

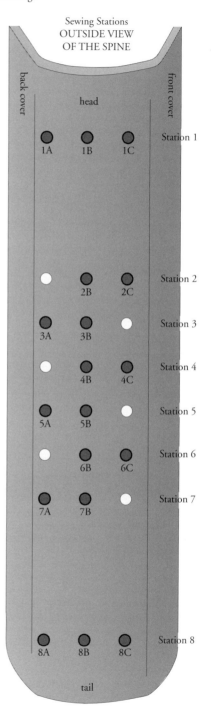

Sewing Stations
OUTSIDE VIEW
OF THE SPINE

Looking at the outside of the cover the stations are numbered from head to tail. They are also lettered from left to right. The third section is sewn onto the *A* stations. The second onto the *B* and the first section uses the *C* stations.

Design your stations on a template cut to the dimensions of the spine. Place a strip of masking tape or white artist's tape the width and length of the spine on the inside of your cover. Transfer the measurements to the tape.

Stations to Be Pierced for the First Sewing

For the first sewing, pierce stations 2*C*, 4*C* and 6*C* on the spine as well as in the first section.

Pierce stations 2*B*–7*B* on the spine as well as in the second section.

Pierce stations 3*A*, 5*A* and 7*A* on the spine as well as in the third section.

Stations to Be Pierced for the Second Sewing

For the second sewing, pierce stations 1*A*, 1*B* and 1*C* on the spine as well as in the book block.

Pierce stations 8*A*, 8*B* and 8*C* on the spine as well as in the book block.

Pierce the stations through the tape for both sewings before starting the first sewing. Remove the tape.

FIRST SEWING

1*a, b* The first sewing is diagrammed on page 222. The darker thread shows the *b* steps. The lighter thread is diagrammed as the *a* steps.
Start on the inside of the third section. Take the needle on the darker *(b)* thread out station 3 of the section and 3*A* of the cover. Take the *a* (lighter color) thread out station 5 and 5*A* of the cover.

2*a*. Set on the second section. Span to station 5*B*. Enter 5*B* of the cover and station 5 of the second section.

2*b*. Span to station 3*B*. Enter 3*B* of the cover and station 3 of the second section. Be careful to keep the stitches tight until the sewing is tied-off.

3*a*. Proceed to station 4 in the second section. Exit station 4 and 4*B* of the cover.

3*b*. Proceed to station 2. Exit station 2 and 2*B* of the cover.

4*a*. Set on the first section. Span to station 4*C*. Enter 4*C* of the cover and station 4 of the first section.

4*b*. Span to station 2*C*. Enter 2*C* of the cover and 2 of the first section. Keep the stitches tight until the sewings are tied-off.

5*b*. Proceed to station 6 in the first section. Exit station 6 and 6*C* of the cover.

5*a*. Tie-off the lighter color thread at station 4 with a half hitch around the darker color thread. make sure all the stitches inside each section are taut before you tie-off.

QUICK Leather Bindings

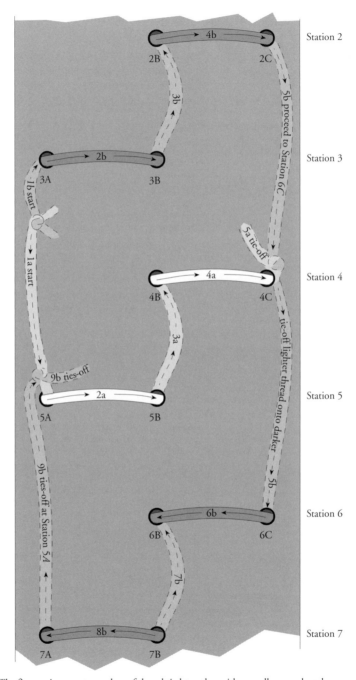

The first sewing uses two colors of thread tied together with a needle on each end.

222

6*b*. Span and enter station 6*B* of the cover and station 6 of the second section.

7*b*. Proceed to station 7. Exit station 7 of the second section and 7*B* of the cover.

8*b*. Span and enter station 7*A* of the cover and station 7 of the third section.

9*b*. Proceed to station 5 in the third section. Tie-off with a half hitch at station 5 around the white thread. Clip the darker dangling thread short.

SECOND SEWING

The second sewing requires three threads of various colors with a needle on each thread. The thread at the *A* stations and third section will be called the *x* thread. The middle thread is *y* and the thread in the first section is *z*.

1*x*. Exit the third section at station 1 through 1*A* of the cover. Wrap around the head to the inside of the same section. Tie-off at station 1.

1*y*. Exit the second section at station 1 and 1*B*. Wrap around the head to the inside. Tie-off at station 1.

1*z*. Exit the first section at station 1 and 1*C*. Wrap around the head to the inside. Tie-off at station 1.

2*x*. Exit station 1 and 1*A* of the cover.

2*y*. Exit station 1 and 1*B* of the cover.

2*z*. Exit station 1 and 1*C* of the cover. Stand the book on a table so both hands are free to form the braided handle.

STARTING THE SECOND SEWING: Three different colors of thread are used with a needle on each thread. Each thread exits a section, goes around the head and ties-off at station 1, then exits that station.

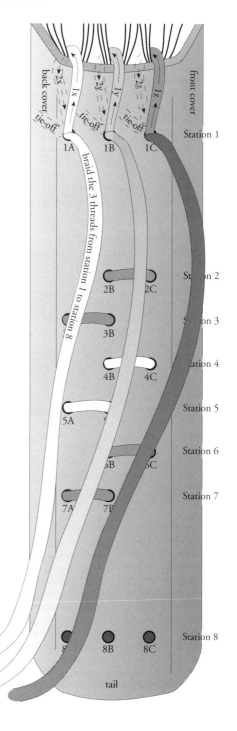

3x, y, z. Braid the three threads until the braid just reaches station 8. Take the *x* thread into station 8*A* of the cover and station 8 of the third section.

Take the *y* thread into station 8*B* of the cover and station 8 of the second section.

Take the *z* thread into station 8*C* of the cover and station 8 of the first section.

4x. Proceed to the tail. Wrap around the tail to the outside of the cover.

5x. Proceed on the spine to station 8*A*. Enter 8*A* of the cover and station 8 of the third section. Tie-off at station 8 with a half hitch.

5y. Proceed on the spine to station 8*B*. Enter 8*B* of the cover and station 8 of the second section. Tie-off at station 8 with a half hitch.

5z. Proceed on the spine to station 8*C*. Enter 8*C* of the cover and station 8 of the first section. Tie-off at station 8 with a half hitch.

The handle will be taut, but will stretch very slightly with use. You can make a longer handle by braiding a few more steps before taking the threads into the cover and the sections.

COMPLETING THE SECOND SEWING:
Step 3 forms the braid down to, or slightly past station 8. Threads are taken inside the cover and sections. Step 4 proceeds to the tail. Step 5 wraps around the tail to the outside and enters station 8. Each thread is tied-off individually inside each section.
Form the braid taut, as it will stretch with use.

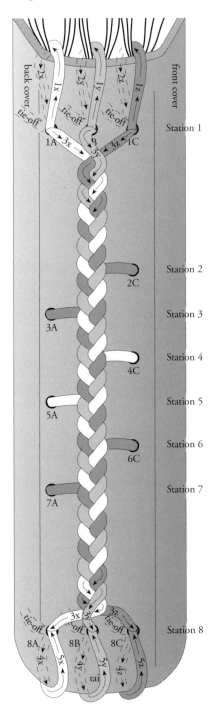

Inside view of the Braided Handle Book I shows the leather hinge and strips of inlaid leather between the turn-ins and the hinge.

After the inside papers were adhered, pencil lines were drawn to extend the lines of the inlaid leather as a means of a visual transition from the leather to the papers.

The spine view of this sewing is shown in color on the back cover of Volume V.

BRAIDED HANDLE BOOK II

The second book with a braided handle also has two sewings. The first sewing attaches the sections to the cover with long stitches.

The second sewing adds the handle in the identical manner as the first book, shown on page 219. The only difference is this one is braided beyond station 8. When the threads are taken to the inside of the book the handle becomes an arch. On the first book the handle is straight and stretched tautly along the spine.

PREPARATION

Prepare a 2-board cover, as described on page 61. Use spine paper which is a stiff paper since you will be stitching around the head and the tail. See page 76.

Thread for the First Sewing

The "first sewing" is actually three separate sewings. Each section is sewn on and tied-off individually.

Threads for the Second Sewing

The second sewing requires three separate threads each with one needle. Length of each thread should be about four times the height of the cover.

Designing the Stations

For the first sewing, there are 8 sewing stations with 3 rows of stations on the spine. All stations are pierced on the spine and in the sections. The second sewing uses stations 1 and 8.

Looking at the outside of the cover the stations are numbered from head to tail. They are also lettered from left to right. The third section is sewn onto the *A* stations. The second onto the *B* stations. The first section uses the *C* stations.

Design your stations on a template cut to the dimensions of the spine. Place a strip of masking tape or white artist's tape the width and length of the spine on the inside of your cover. Transfer the measurements to the tape.

Pierce the stations through the tape before starting the first sewing. Remove the tape. Pierce the sections.

FIRST SEWING

Before starting the sewing, read the note on page 230.

1. Set on the first section to be sewn. The diagram is for the third section down the *A* stations. Exit station 1 of the section and 1*A* of the cover.
2. Proceed to station 2. Enter station 2*A* of the cover and 2 of the section.
3. Tie a knot at station 2.
4. Proceed inside the section to station 3. Exit station 3 of the section and 3*A* of the cover.

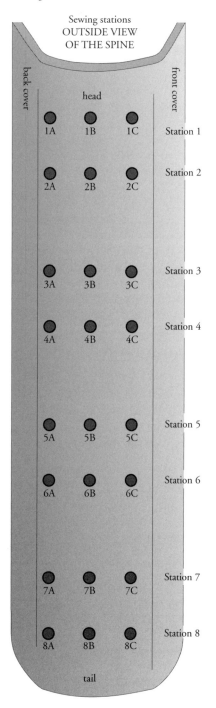

Sewing stations
OUTSIDE VIEW
OF THE SPINE

back cover

front cover

head

1A	1B	1C	Station 1
2A	2B	2C	Station 2
3A	3B	3C	Station 3
4A	4B	4C	Station 4
5A	5B	5C	Station 5
6A	6B	6C	Station 6
7A	7B	7C	Station 7
8A	8B	8C	Station 8

tail

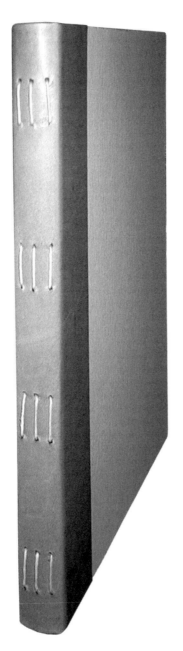

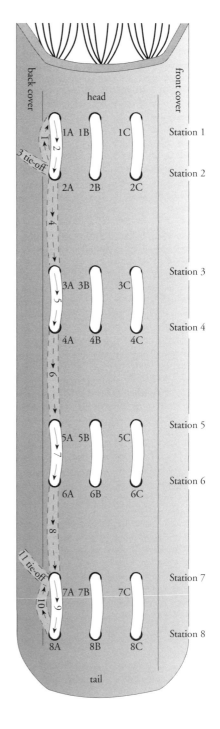

The "first sewing" is actually 3 separate sewings. Each section is sewn onto the cover individually with a running stitch.

5. Proceed on the spine to station 4. Enter station 4*A* of the cover and 4 of the section.

6. Proceed to station 5 and exit.

7. Proceed on the spine to station 6. Enter station 6*A* of the cover and 6 of the section.

8. Proceed inside the section to station 7. Exit station 7 of the section and 7*A* of the cover.

9. Proceed on the spine to station 8. Enter station 8*A* of the cover and 8 of the section.

10. Proceed inside to station 7.

11. Tie-off inside the section with a half hitch at station 7.

Sew the remaining two sections in the same manner.

SECOND SEWING

The second sewing is identical to the second sewing of the Braided Handle Book I. See instructions beginning on page 223.

NOTE: Half the ties-off can be eliminated by tying the threads for the first sewing to the threads used for the braiding in the second sewing.

The knot connecting the two threads for each section should be a weaver's knot. It would be at station 1 on the inside of each section. Allow the longer thread for the braiding to remain inside the section while the shorter thread is used to form the running stitch of the first sewing. Do not tie-off the first sewing until the second sewing is completed. Tie-off both sewings with a square knot at station 8.

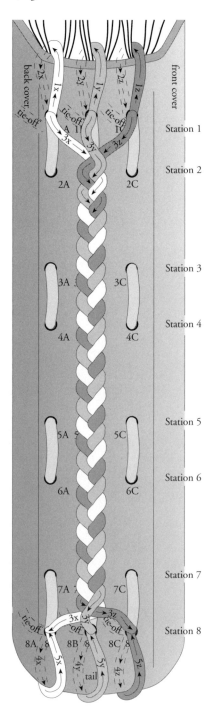

230

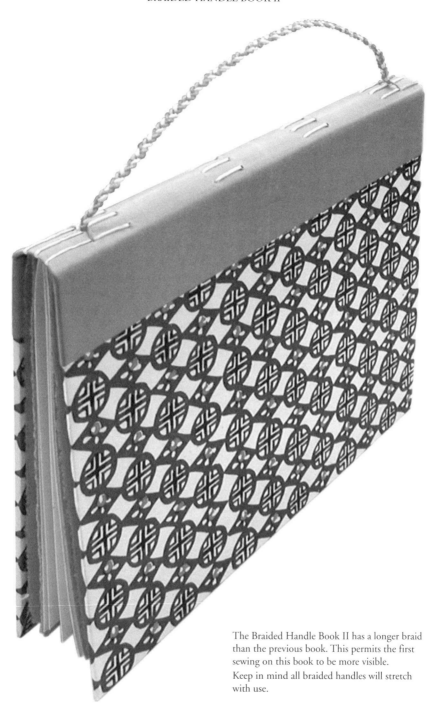

The Braided Handle Book II has a longer braid than the previous book. This permits the first sewing on this book to be more visible.

Keep in mind all braided handles will stretch with use.

BRAIDED HANDLE BOOK III

BELLA'S BRAIDED BIRTHDAY BOOK

As the braided handle books evolved, this third design became Bella's birthday book. Book cloth was used since she is vegetarian. Rather than quarter cloth, I made a full cloth cover in an attempt to protect the corners of the covers at the foredge.

This was my first full cloth cover using the positionable mounting adhesive. The corners upholstered easily. Do not attempt a half or full leather binding with unpared leather.

Besides a sketch book, I thought I ought to give her another present. I decided to give Bella her own word square, so I made one up shortly after sewing the book, but prior to adding the decorative papers. It will be printed on paper and adhered to the cover. Lilacs were in bloom, so that word found its way into her square.

Braided Handle Book III was designed for the second birthday of Isabella Punzi-Watts.

PREPARATION

Prepare a 2-board cover, as described on page 61. Use spine paper which is stiff since you will be stitching around the head and the tail.

Threads for the First Sewing

The first sewing uses two colors of thread tied together at one end so it appears to be one length of thread with a knot in the middle. Clip the shorter ends of thread close to the knot. Smash the knot so it does not bulge. I suggest you use a weaver's knot instead of a square knot as it has less bulk.

Place a needle on each end as this is a 2-needle sewing. This thread should be about twice the height of the cover.

Threads for the Second Sewing

The second sewing requires three separate threads each with one needle. Length of each thread should be about four times the height of the cover.

Designing the Stations

There are 6 stations in 3 rows on the spine. All 18 stations are pierced on the spine. All 6 stations are pierced in each of the sections.

Looking at the outside of the cover the stations are numbered from head to tail. They are also lettered from left to right. The third section is sewn onto the *A* stations. The second onto the *B* and the first section uses the *C* stations.

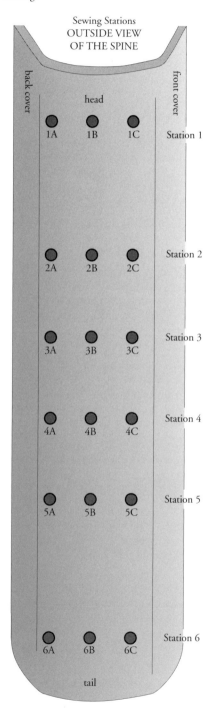

Sewing Stations
OUTSIDE VIEW
OF THE SPINE

back cover

front cover

head

1A 1B 1C — Station 1

2A 2B 2C — Station 2

3A 3B 3C — Station 3

4A 4B 4C — Station 4

5A 5B 5C — Station 5

6A 6B 6C — Station 6

tail

Design your stations on a template which is the dimensions of the spine. Place a strip of masking tape or white artist's tape the width and length of the spine on the inside of your cover. Transfer the measurements to the tape.

Pierce all the stations through the tape before starting the first sewing. Remove the tape. Pierce the sections.

FIRST SEWING

1*a, b* The darker thread shows the *b* steps. The lighter thread is diagrammed as the *a* steps.

Start on the inside of the third section. Take the needle on the darker *(b)* thread out station 2 of the section and 2*A* of the cover. Take the *a* (lighter color) thread out station 3 and 3*A* of the cover.

2*a.* Set on the second section. Span to station 3*B*. Enter 3*B* of the cover and station 3 of the second section.

2*b.* Span to station 2*B*. Enter 2*B* of the cover and station 2 of the second section. Keep the stitches tight until the sewing is tied-off.

3*a.* Proceed to station 2 in the second section. Exit station 2 and 2*B* of the cover.

3*b.* Proceed to station 3 in the second section. Exit station 3 and 3*B* of the cover.

4*a.* Set on the first section. Span to station 2*C*. Enter 2*C* of the cover and station 2 of the first section.

The first sewing is a 2-needle sewing. It attaches the book block to the cover in the middle of the spine. Two colors of thread are tied together. A needle is placed on the end of each color.

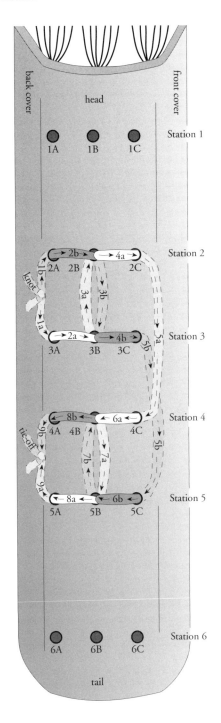

4b. Span to station 3C. Enter 3C of the cover and station 3 of the first section.

5a. Proceed to station 4 in the first section. Exit station 4 and 4C of the cover.

5b. Proceed to station 5 in the first section. Exit station 5 and 5C of the cover.

6a. Span to station 4B. Enter 4B of the cover and station 4 of the second section.

6b. Span to station 5B. Enter 5B of the cover and station 5 of the second section.

7a. Proceed to station 5 in the second section. Exit station 5 and 5B of the cover.

7b. Proceed to station 4 in the second section. Exit station 4 and 4B of the cover.

8a. Span to station 5A. Enter 5A of the cover and station 5 of the third section.

8b. Span to station 4A. Enter 4A of the cover and station 4 of the third section.

9a, b. Tie the two dandling threads inside the third section together with a square knot at either station 4 or station 5. Clip the loose ends.

SECOND SEWING

The second sewing is identical to the second sewing of the Braided Handle Book I, except instead of entering station 8 at the tail, enter at station 6. See instructions beginning on page 223.

The second sewing forms the braided handle.

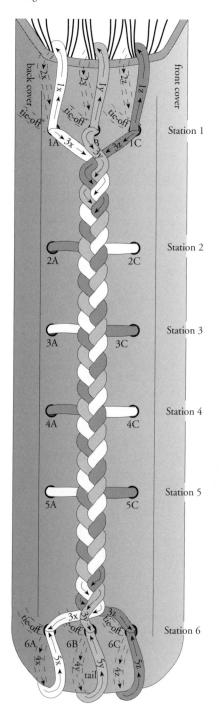

236

The first sewing has been completed. Holes for the second sewing were pre-pierced and can be seen near the head and tail.

With the Italian inside papers, the cover is completed. Stations are pierced in the spine and the book block. Below is the template used for designing the stations. I do not use tape on the spine but hold the scrap paper template firmly in place and pierce through it and the spine. Without tape, piercing must be done with great care so the template does not slip. The result would be holes that do not line up.

The Braided Handle Book III is complete are ready for the artist's drawings. A picture of Bella with her book is on page 274.

4-SECTION

SPIRALLING THREADS

INTRODUCTION

In Volume II Non-Adhesive Binding I limited the structures to 1, 2 or 3 section bindings. In Volume V I want to create a couple new bindings for books containing from 1 to 8 sections. I think that gives a broad range in the number of pages for these quick leather bindings. For 4-section bindings I will describe two. The first will be called *Spiralling Threads.*

Often in designing a sewing I like to have vertical threads which go around the head and tail. Looking at the closed book from the foredge to the spine, the threads give a slight suggestion of endbands.

Looking at the spine on the shelf I enjoy counting the number of threads going around the head or tail revealing the number of sections in that particular book.

My introduction to the use of threads extending around the head and tail was when Gary Frost introduced me to an ancient binding titled Long Stitch through Slotted Wrapper Cover. I described it in Volume I.

The second influence in designing this sewing comes from three sewings created for Volume II: *Barber Pole, Coiled Line* and *Coil Spring.* Although the more I look at it, this new sewing is more related to Tacket Bindings illustrated in the latest Volume I. Tacket bindings solidly pack the vertical stitch. Betsy Palmer Eldridge says they are perhaps 16th century German.

Title for this binding comes from twisting contrasting color threads as the long stitches on the spine. Four threads on the spine extend around the head and tail to the inside of each of the four sections. This sewing is shown in color on the back cover of Volume V.

Color Threads

Contrasting colors of thread are used. The prototype uses four colors:
• A light and dark color for sections 1 and 4;
• A different light and dark color for sections 2 and 3.

If you wish, you can limit the sewing to 2 colors, one light and one dark, for each of the four sections.

Sewing Stations

Stations are numbered and lettered on the spine. The sections are only numbered. Looking from the outside in the photo to the right, the fourth section sews onto the *D* stations, the third onto the *C*s, the second onto the *B*s and the first onto the *A* stations.

Stations 1*B* and 1*C* are positioned farther down from the head than 1*A* and 1*D* to give longer stitches in the center for the design. The same is true with 12*B* and 12*C* at the tail.

For the first and fourth sections and cover, piece stations 1, 2, 3, 6, 7, 10, 11 and 12.

For the second and third sections and cover, piece stations 1, 4, 5, 8, 9 and 12.

NOTE: The spine paper was not stiff enough for this sewing. The leather is kinked at the tail. Whenever you sew around the head and tail you must use a rather stiff spine paper the height of the boards.

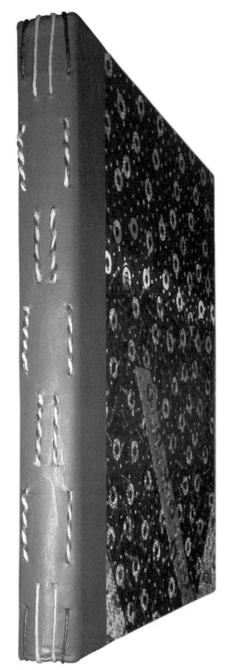

Spiralling Threads is a 4-section sewing with quarter kangaroo leather.

242

SPIRALLING THREADS

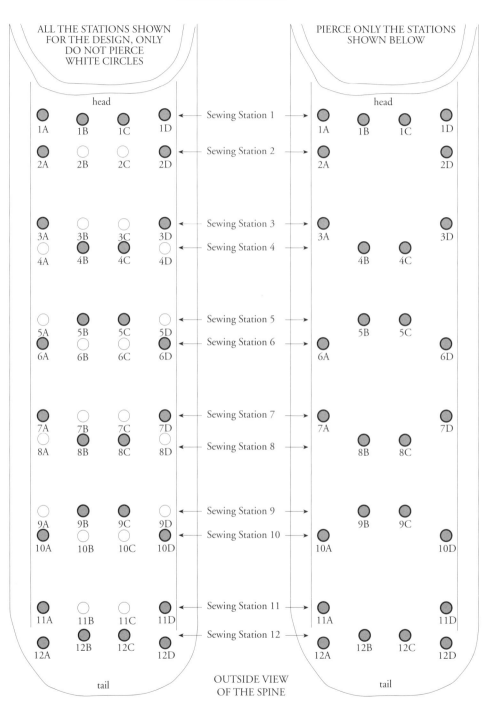

ALL THE STATIONS SHOWN
FOR THE DESIGN, ONLY
DO NOT PIERCE
WHITE CIRCLES

PIERCE ONLY THE STATIONS
SHOWN BELOW

head

head

← Sewing Station 1 →
← Sewing Station 2 →
← Sewing Station 3 →
← Sewing Station 4 →
← Sewing Station 5 →
← Sewing Station 6 →
← Sewing Station 7 →
← Sewing Station 8 →
← Sewing Station 9 →
← Sewing Station 10 →
← Sewing Station 11 →
← Sewing Station 12 →

tail

tail

OUTSIDE VIEW
OF THE SPINE

243

SEWING PROCEDURE
Adding the Threads to Be Twisted

Sew the book standing on a table at shoulder height to control twisting the threads and to leave both hands free to twist the threads.

All four sections are sewn separately. For the first and fourth sections the darker color threads extend around the head and tail. The lighter color threads extend around the ends in the second and third sections. If you wish you can use only the darker or lighter threads extending around the head and tail. It doesn't matter structurally; it is a design decision.

Before sewing the sections, the threads *not* used to extend around the head and tail will be attached to the cover, only.

For the first and fourth section cut a length of lighter color thread approximately 4 times the height of the spine. Place a needle on each end.

Start on the inside of the cover. Exit with one needle out station 2 *A*. Take the other needle out station 2*D*. Center the threads dangling on the spine.

For the second and third section cut a length of darker color thread 4 times the height of the spine. Place a needle on each end.

Start on the inside of the cover. Exit with one needle out station 4*B*. Take the other needle out station 4*C*. Center these threads. There are now 4 threads dangling on the spine.

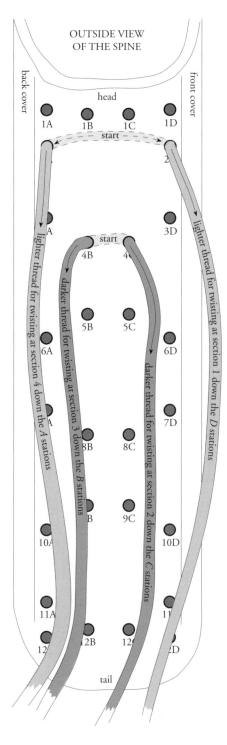

244

Sewing the First Section

Place the first section inside to the far left next to the front cover. This section will line up with the D stations, since the lettering of stations is from left to right on the outside of the spine. This first section soon will be sewn down the D stations with a darker thread.

Grasp the threads on the spine which hang from the A, B and C stations. Place them on the inside, between the back cover and the section. This leaves only the thread dangling from station 2D.

Threads for twisting, illustrated on the facing page, which extend from stations 2A, 4B and 4C are temporarily pulled over the top to the inside of the back cover to be out of the way until the sections with those lettered stations are sewn.

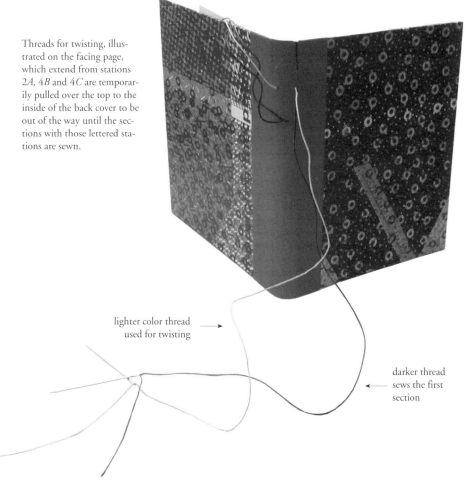

lighter color thread → used for twisting

darker thread ← sews the first section

A lighter color thread has exited station 2A and 2D *of* the cover, only before the section is added. A darker thread exits 4A and 4D. The first section is added. A new thread of darker color exists station 1 of the section and 1D of the cover and climbs over the head as stated in step 1 at the top of the page.

1. Cut a darker thread which is 2 1/2 times the height of the cover. Place a needle on one end. Take the needle out station 1 of the section and 1D of the cover. Pull all the thread to the outside except for a small amount. Proceed on the spine to the head. Wrap the thread around the head to the inside of the section. Proceed inside the section to station 1.

2. Tie a square knot with the dangling thread. Clip the shorter thread to 1/2″. Make sure the stitch on the spine is vertical and taut, but not so tight as to crimp the leather.

3. Proceed inside the section to station 2. Exit station 2 of the section and 2D of the cover. Be careful not to pierce the dangling lighter thread. Pull all the thread to the outside so the stitch inside the section (step 3) is taut.

4. With one hand grasp the lighter and darker threads close to station 2D. Twist in either direction about 180°. Hold this position with that hand while with the other hand grab the dangling threads and rotate them 180° so that they pass over your wrist to keep them from tangling as you continue to twist.

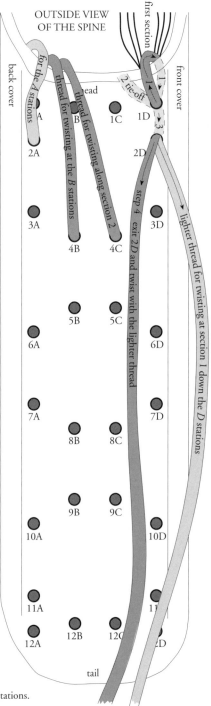

Starting to sew the first section down the D stations.

With the hand grasping the threads continue to twist another 180°. With the other hand, flip the dangling threads over your wrist. Continue twisting in the is manner until the 2-ply thread twisted extends to station 3D.

Hold the end of the twist with thumb and forefinger of one hand so it does not untwist. With the other hand take one needle through station 3D of the cover and 3 of the section to the inside. Pull almost all the thread to the inside but leave a little slack on the twisted threads.

Take the other needle to the inside at the same station. Gently pull on both threads inside until the twisted threads on the spine are taut. The twisting should be uniform in tension so that an equal amount of both the lighter and darker threads are seen and the angle and shape of the twisting is uniform.

5. Pick up one of the needles. Proceed on the inside and exit station 6 of the section and 6D of the cover. Take the remaining thread on the inside out station 6 of the section and 6D of the cover. Be sure not to pierce the other thread.

Sewing the first section down the D stations. Compare this illustration with the photo on the following page.

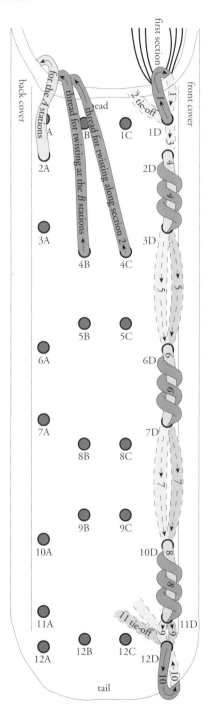

6. Twist the two threads in the manner described in step 4. Hold the twist while one needle enters station 7D of the cover and station 7 of the section.Bring the other needle to the inside at station 7.
7. Proceed on the inside and exit station 10 of the section and 10D of the cover. Take the remaining thread to the outside at station 10 and 10D
8. Twist the two threads. Brings the two needles to the inside at station 11D of the cover and station 11 of the section.
9. Take the darker thread and exit station 12 of the section and 12D of the cover.
10. Proceed on the outside of the spine to the tail. Wrap around the tail to the inside of the section.
11. Proceed inside to station 12. Tie-off with a square knot with the lighter thread precisely at station 12. Do not make the knot so tight that it crimps the leather at the tail. Clip both threads to about 1/2".

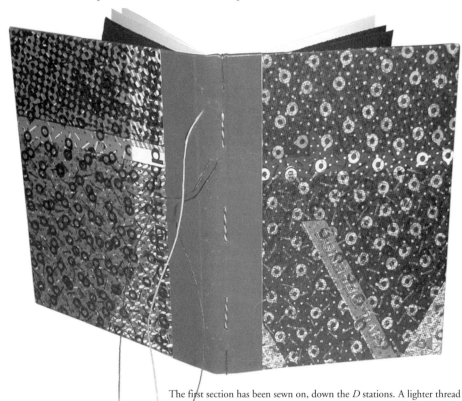

The first section has been sewn on, down the *D* stations. A lighter thread will now be used to sew the second section down the *C* stations using the darker thread extending from station 4*C* to do the twists.
Paper for the covers are make-readies from *Civil Defense* by Philip Zimmermann, published offset by Space Heater Multiples, 1983, 1984.

Sewing the Second Section

Grasp the darker thread on the spine which extends from station 4C. Pull it from the inside of the back cover out onto the spine ready for twisting. Take a length of lighter color of thread which is 2 1/2 times the height of the cover. Add a needle to one end.

Each section is sewn the same as the first, only the second and third sections exit and enter different numbered stations.

1. Start on the inside. Exit station 1 of the second section and 1C of the cover.

   Pull most of the thread to the outside. Proceed on the spine to the head. Wrap the thread around the head to the inside of the second section.

   Proceed inside the section to station 1.

2. Tie a square knot with the dangling thread. Clip the shorter thread to 1/2".

3. Proceed inside the section to station 4. Exit station 4 of the section and 4C of the cover. Pull all the thread to the outside so the stitch inside the section is taut.

4. Twist the two threads extending from station 4C the same number of twists as with the first section, if you have made the distance from station 4 to 5 the same distance as from stations 2 to 3. Take the two needles to the inside at station 5C.

Sewing the first section down the D stations. Compare this illustration with the photo on the following page.

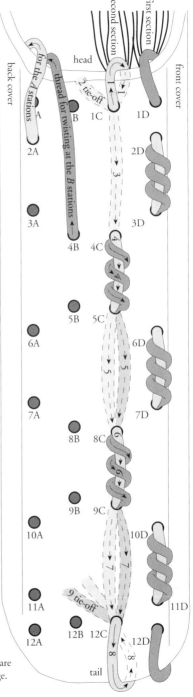

249

5. Proceed on the inside. Exit station 8 of the section and 8 *C* of the cover with one needle. Take the remaining thread out this same station.

6. Twist the two threads. Enter with one needle at station 9 *C* of the cover and station 9 of the section. Bring the other needle to the inside at this station.

7. Proceed with the light color thread on the inside to station 12. Exit station 12 of the section and 12 *C* of the cover with the light thread, only.

8. Proceed on the spine to the tail. Wrap around the tail to the inside of the section.

9. Proceed inside to station 12. Tie-off with a square knot with the darker thread at station 12. Clip both threads to about 1/2″.

Sewing the Third Section

Sew the third section in the same manner as the first using the same numbered stations, but at letter *B* stations.

Sewing the Fourth Section

Sew the fourth section in the same manner as the second using the same numbered stations, but at letter *A* stations.

The binding called Spiralling Threads is completed. Black pages are smaller than the white.

Four threads can be seen wrapping around the tail of the spine. Each thread goes to the inside of one of the four sections of the book block.

This is the inside cover of the book shown on on the facing page. Dark calf is used for the quarter leather and inside leather/hinge. A light color thread is inlaid in the seams between the turn-ins and the inside leather. See: *Optional Inlaid Threads,* page 86.

HASH MARKS

This is an elegant binding that can have as many rows of hash marks as you wish. The example to the right requires 22 sewing stations which yields 11 rows of hash marks. It would be difficult to diagram that many stations. The description will be limited to 14 stations and 7 rows of hash marks. A photo illustration of that book is on page 259.

Each row of stitches can slant forward or backward. The example to the right has 2 rows slanting backward at the head and tail. The description will diagram 1 row at the head and tail which will slant backward. With a little sketching and forethought you can design your book to have as many rows of hash marks as desired, and slant each row forward or backward.

Since there are 3 hash marks per row, I tend to be fooled into thinking this is a 3-section sewing until I count the number of sewing stations.

NOTE: Don't guess when you sew this one. You cannot know intuitively which station to exit inside the sections. This sewing requires following the written instructions, much like landing a plane via instruments than by sight.

The Hash Marks style requires a lot of attention to know which station and section to enter and which station to exit. But the effort is worth it. This is one of the nicer sewings in Volume V.

This binding is reproduced on the front cover of Volume V.

Sewing Stations

Cut a strip of paper the height and width of the spine. Mark out a grid in pencil for as many numbered stations as you will need. There are 14 in this description. Mark in pencil all 4 lettered stations for each row, even though you will pierce only 3 lettered stations.

In designing the stations, remember the section is not as tall as the cover. Make sure station 1 is far enough away from the head of the cover to catch the section. Make sure the final row of stations is up from the tail so that it will set in on the section.

Using this grid, lay the paper on the inside of the leather spine. Pierce through the paper guide and through the leather spine. Pierce all the stations needed.

In this description, you will pierce
stations 1*B, C* and *D*
stations 2*A, B* and *C*
stations 3*A, B* and *C*
stations 4*B, C* and *D*
stations 5*A, B* and *C*
stations 6*B, C* and *D*
stations 7*A, B* and *C*
stations 8*B, C* and *D*
stations 9*A, B* and *C*
stations 10*B, C* and *D*
stations 11*A, B* and *C*
stations 12*B, C* and *D*
stations 13*B, C* and *D*
stations 14*A, B* and *C.*

SEWING STATIONS: The grid shows all of the 4 lettered stations for each of the 14 numbered stations. However, pierce only 3 lettered stations in each row.

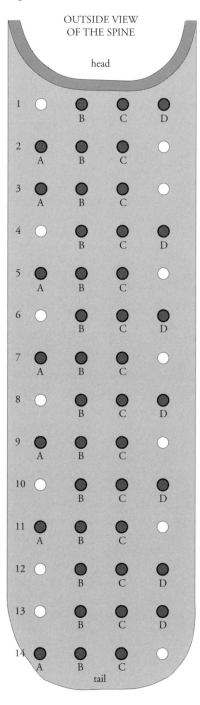

OUTSIDE VIEW
OF THE SPINE

head

tail

SEWING PROCEDURE

Sewing the First Two Sections

The "first two" sections to be sewn will be the final section in the book block and the next to last.

1. Set on the final section lined up with the *A* stations on the cover. Exit station 14 of the section and 14*A* of the cover.

2. Set on the next to last section. Angle and enter station 13*B* of the cover into station 13 of the next to last section.

3. Proceed inside the section. Exit station 12 of the section and 12*B* of the cover.

4. Angle and enter 11*A* of the cover into station 11 of the final section.

5. Tighten the stitches on the spine. Tie a square knot with the dangling thread inside the final section at station 11.

6. Proceed to station 9 and exit 9 and 9*A* of the cover.

7. Angle towards the tail and enter station 10*B* of the cover into station 10 of the next to last section.

8. Proceed inside the section towards the head. Skip station 9 and exit station 8 and 8*B* of the cover.

9. Angle towards the head. Enter station 7*A* of the cover into station 7 of final section.

10. Exit station 5 of the section and 5*A* of the cover.

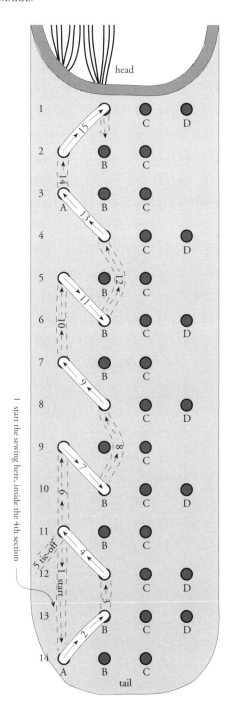

255

11. Angle towards the tail and enter station 6B of the cover into station 6 of the next to last section.

12. Proceed inside the section towards the head. Skip station 5 and exit station 4 and 4B of the cover.

13. Angle towards the head. Enter station 3A of the cover into station 3 of the final section.

14. Proceed to station 2 and exit 2 of the section and 2A of the cover.

15. Angle towards the head. Enter station 1B of the cover into station 1 of the next to last section.

Sewing the Middle Two Sections

All four sections are sewn with a single thread. The sewing continues with step 16. The next to last section, from here on will be referred to as the *third section.*

The second section in the book block will be called the *second section.*

16. Proceed toward the tail in the third section. Exit station 2 and 2B of the cover.

17. Set on the second section. Angle right and enter station 1C of the cover and station 1 of the second section.

18. Proceed to station 4, skipping stations 2 and 3. Exit 4 and station 4C of the cover.

19. Angle left and enter 3B of the cover into station 3 of the third section.

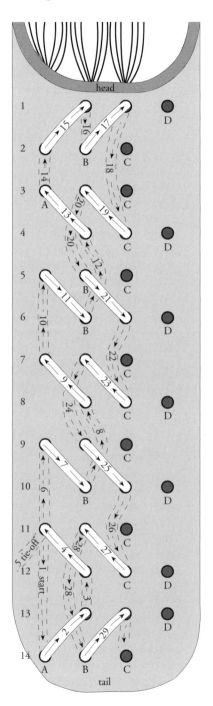

20. Exit station 5 and 5*B* of the cover.

21. Angle right and enter station 6*C* of the cover and station 6 of the second section.

22. Skip 7 and exit station 8 and 8*C* of the cover.

23. Angle left and enter 7*B* and station 7 of the third section.

24. Skip 8 and exit station 9 and 9*B* of the cover.

25. Angle right and enter station 10*C* of the cover and station 10 of the second section.

26. Exit 12 and 12C of the cover.

27. Angle left and enter 11*B* and 11 of the third section.

28. Skip 12 and 13. Proceed to 14. Exit 14 and 14*B*.

29. Angle and enter 13*C* and 13.

Sewing the Final Two Sections

The final two sections to be sewn are the first and second sections of the book. The sewing continues with step 30.

30. Proceed in the second section to 14*C*. Exit 14 and 14*C*.

31. Set on the first section. Angle and enter 13*D* into station 13 of the first section.

32. Proceed to station 12. Exit 12 and 12*D* of the cover.

33. Angle and enter 11*C* and station 11 of the second section.

34. Proceed to and exit station 9 and 9*C* of the cover.

35. Angle and enter 10*D* and station 10 of the first section.

36. Proceed to and exit station 8 and 8*D* of the cover.

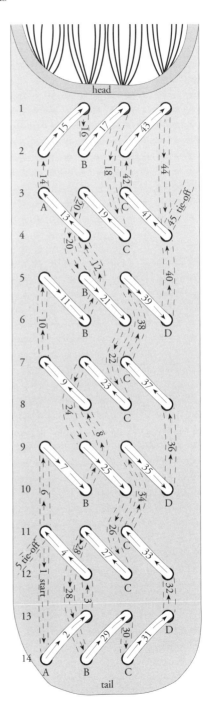

37. Angle and enter 7*C* and station 7 of the second section.
38. Proceed to and exit station 5 and 5*C* of the cover.
39. Angle and enter 6*D* and station 6 of the first section.
40. Proceed to and exit station 4 and 4*D* of the cover.
41. Angle and enter 3*C* and station 3 of the second section.
42. Proceed to and exit station 2 and 2*C* of the cover.
43. Angle and enter 1*D* and station 1 of the first section.
44. Proceed on the inside of the first section to station 3.
45. Tie-off with a half hitch with the stitch at station 3.

OUTSIDE VIEW OF THE SPINE:
This is the same drawing as on the previous page. It is repeated so you won't have to fan the pages to follow the diagrams.

This of Hash Marks binding uses only 14 sewing stations, the same number as in the written description. The only difference is I forgot to flip the template over when I was piercing the stations, so the hash marks are the reverse of what I had intended. I had to flip the diagrams and hold them up to the light in order to follow the sewing path!

This binding is the same dimensions as the book shown on page 253. In fact, all the boards and sections for the prototypes in Volume V were pre-cut to the same dimensions when I started writing the book.

The sewing shown to the right makes a good looking binding. I kept the spine flat by reinforcing with a rather stiff paper before adding the hinge, as opposed to thinner paper for the round-looking spine on page 253.

I prefer the more rounded look of the sewing shown on page 253 and its 22 stations gives a textured as well as patterned spine. The sewing on the right is reproduced in color on the back cover of Volume V.

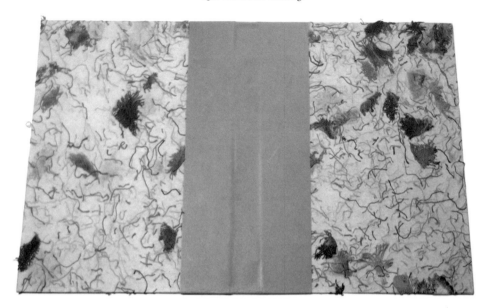

ABOVE: The quarter leather is kangaroo. The boards are covered with Thai Cal Ling Autumn paper which contains pieces of cloth.

BELOW: Turn-ins have been made. Strips of Japanese dragonfly paper extend the lines of the inlaid leather. The bare board is visible as the inside papers of lightweight Thai National Mulberry Paper have not been added to the boards.

All the papers in this binding, and in most of the bindings in Volume V, are available from Hollander's in Ann Arbor. See page 27 for the address and online site.

ABOVE: The inside papers have been added to the boards. Mulberry paper was used as it is translucent and gives a hint of the underlying strips of Japanese dragonfly paper.
BELOW: The sewing is completed.

ALTERNATING LONG STITCH

This sewing probably looks familiar. It is my modification of the Long Stitch through Slotted Wrapper Cover which is described in Volume I.

Threads on the spine remain parallel, unlike the traditional binding. The first, third and fifth sections have longer stitches which wrap around the head and tail. This gives not quite an imbricated pattern, nor brick, but I am sure there is some name for the patterning. It looks good, anyhow.

More importantly, even though there are more sections, it sews faster than any of the 4-section sewings devised for Volume V. A single thread is used in this 1-needle sewing.

Preparation

Determine the length of the stitches you wish on the spine. I have kept the shorter stitches of uniform length at 3/8″. The longer stitches ar 11/4″, except for those at the head and tail. The three longer stitches at the head are 3/4″ while those at the tail are 1″. I prefer slightly longer stitches at the tail to suggest a base. I think the sewing is more pleasing than if all the long stitches were exactly the same length.

Sewing Stations

Once the spine is designed, cut a piece of paper or masking tape the dimensions of the spine with the stations drawn on it. Place the drawing on the inside of the cover. Place the cover on a self seal cutting mat. Slit the 8 cover stations through the pattern.

Mark 10 stations for the sections. See the diagram on the following page.

Alternating Long Stitch is a 5–section sewing.

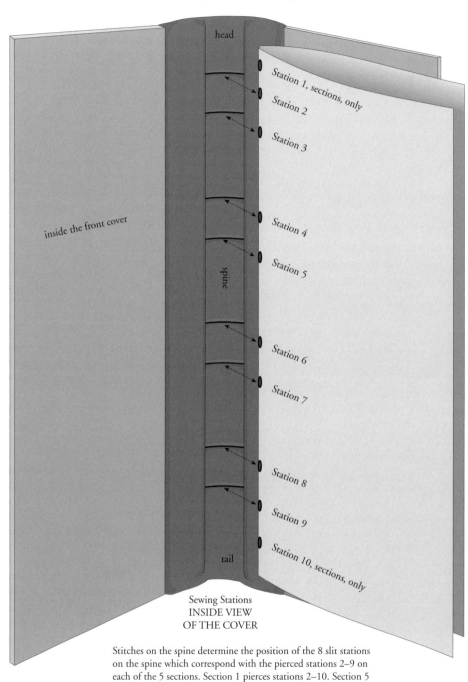

head

Station 1, sections, only

Station 2

Station 3

inside the front cover

Station 4

Station 5

spine

Station 6

Station 7

Station 8

Station 9

Station 10, sections, only

tail

Sewing Stations
INSIDE VIEW
OF THE COVER

Stitches on the spine determine the position of the 8 slit stations on the spine which correspond with the pierced stations 2–9 on each of the 5 sections. Section 1 pierces stations 2–10. Section 5 pierces 1–9. The middle three sections pierce all 10 stations.

SEWING PROCEDURE

Sewing the First Section

On the outside of the spine the sewing proceeds from right to left, from the first to the final section of the book block.

1. Start on the inside of the first section. Exit station 2. Take the needle through the slit at station 2 all the way to the right of the slit close to the front cover. Proceed to the head. Wrap around the head to the inside of the section close to the hinge-fold. Proceed to station 2.

2. Tie-off with a square knot right at station 2. Clip the shorter thread so it does not extend beyond the book. Steps 3–9 form what is referred to as a *running stitch,* sewing in and out of each successive station:

3. Proceed to station 3. Exit station 3 of the section and the slit in the cover. Pull down lightly and it should align the thread extending from the slit so it is close to the hinge-fold.

4. Proceed on the spine to station 4. Enter station 4 of the slit and the section forming a *long stitch* on the spine.

5. Proceed inside to station 5. Exit station 5 of the section and the slit in the cover.

6. Proceed to station 6. Enter station 6 of the slit and the section.

7. Proceed inside to station 7. Exit station 7 of the section and the slit in the cover.

8. Proceed to station 8. Enter station 8 of the slit and the section.

9. Proceed inside to station 9. Exit station 9 of the section and the slit in the cover.

10. Proceed to the tail. Wrap around to the inside of the section. Go to station 10. Exit the section, only, at station 10. Set on the next section to be sewn.

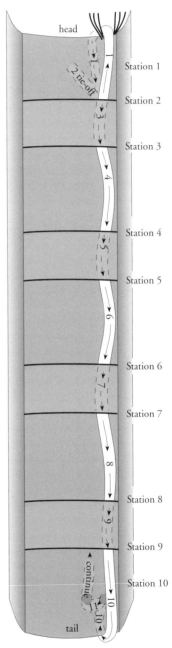

OUTSIDE VIEW OF THE SPINE: Sewing the first section of the book block

Sewing the Second Section

11. Enter the next section, only, from the mountain peak to the valley at station 10. Position this section next to the first.

12. Proceed inside the new section to station 9. Exit station 9 and the slit of the cover, 2/5 the distance across the spine. If you exit too close to the thread in step 10, your sections will all be bunched towards the front cover rather than evenly spaced across the spine.

13–19. Form a running stitch, sewing in and out of each successive station towards the head. Step 19 enters the slit at station 2 and the section.

20. Proceed on the inside the section to station 1. Exit the section, only.

Sewing the Third Section

21. Set on the third section. Enter the new section, only, from the mountain peak to the valley at station 1. Center this section on the spine.

22. Proceed to the head, Wrap around the head to the outside of the spine.

23. Proceed to station 2. Enter the slit and the section at station 2.

24–30. Form a running stitch, sewing towards the tail. Step 30 exits the section and the slit at station 9.

31. Proceed on the spine around the tail to the inside the section to station 10. Exit the section, only.

Sewing the Fourth Section

32. Set on the fourth section. Enter the new section, only, from the mountain peak to the valley at station 10.

33. Proceed to station 9. Exit the section and the slit at station 9.

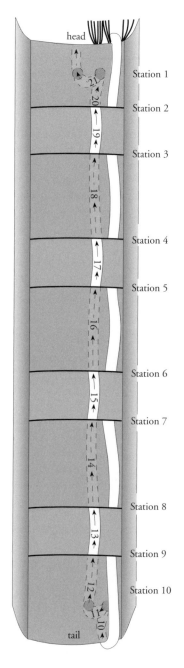

Sewing the second section of the book block

266

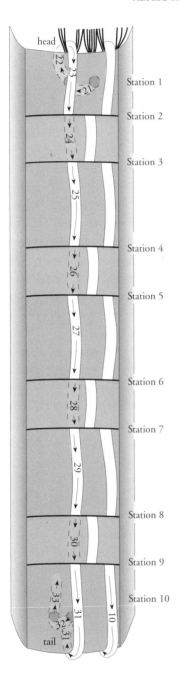

Sewing the third section of
the book block

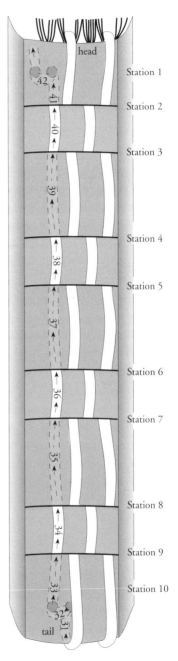

Sewing the fourth section of
the book block

34–40. Form a running stitch towards the head. Step 40 enters the slit at station 2 and enters the section.

41. Proceed inside the section to station 1. Exit the section, only.

Sewing the Fifth Section

42. Set on the fifth section. Enter the final section, only, from the mountain peak to the valley at station 1.

43. Proceed to the head, Wrap around the head to the outside of the spine.

44. Proceed to station 2. Enter the slit and the section at station 2.

45–51. Form a running stitch, sewing towards the tail. Step 51 exits the section and the slit at station 9.

52. Proceed on the spine to the tail. Wrap around the tail to the inside the final section.

53. Proceed to station 9.

54. Tie-off inside the section with a half hitch.

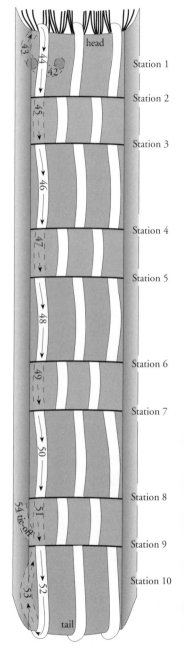

Sewing the fifth section of the book block

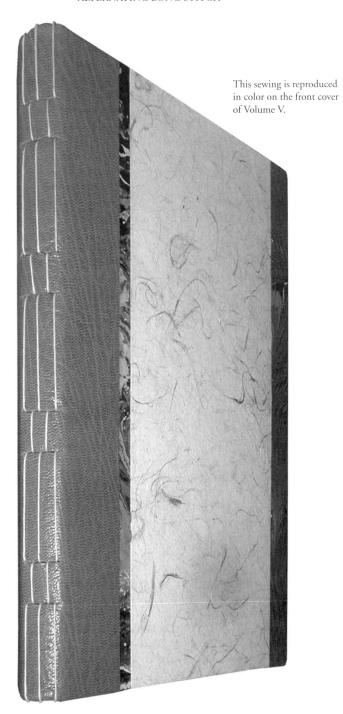

This sewing is reproduced
in color on the front cover
of Volume V.

Like the Long Stitch through Slotted Wrapper Cover, which is described in Volume I, this Alternating Long Stitch sews quickly. It is an elegant quarter leather binding which can serve many purposes.

Above: Stitches seen inside the first, third and fifth sections come around the head and tail.
Below: Strips of darker kangaroo leather are inlaid between the turn-ins at the head and tail and the leather hinge.

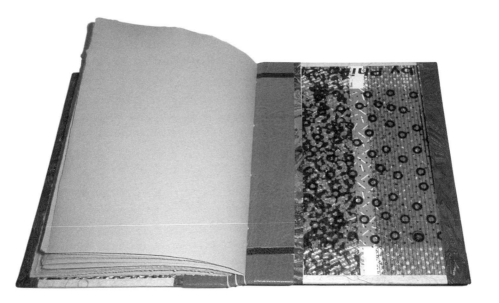

CONCLUSION

Maybe it comes with practice, but this book was a sheer joy to write, to make
up the sewings, photograph them and to draw the diagrams. I think in
part it's because I have always wanted to create a bunch of hard cover
bindings that have from 4 to about 100 pages. These are the size
books I need for most of my own work. I don't need rounded
and backed books of several hundred pages. The icing on
the cake is that these hard cover books can be cloth
bindings or quarter leather with leather hinges
inside. That is exciting to me because I have
eliminated most of the steps traditional
binders would undertake, reducing
the process to the bare necessi-
ties.

Now that you have
bound a couple of these
books you see what I
mean. These are really
quick leather bindings.

keith a. smith
20 May 2002

Bella's braided birthday book
designed for Isabella Punzi-Watts
is described beginning on page 233.

POSTSCRIPT:

STAPLED BOOKS

INTRODUCTION

post•script n. Abbr. **P.S., p.s., PS**

1. A message appended at the end of a letter after the writer's signature.
2. Additional information appended to the manuscript, as of a book or an article.
   [Medieval Latin *postscriptum*, from neuter past participle of Latin *postscribere*, to write after : *post-*, post- + *scribere*, to write.]

Postscript these days is also a kind of computer language into which text and pictures are translated before sending the book on disk to the printers.

I have a few extra pages in Volume V so I will include my staple binding here since there was not room for it in Volume IV. It would have been more appropriate in the last book since it is a single sheet binding.

Actually, it was not appropriate, as every single sheet binding in Volume IV opens flat, whereas the stapled binding stabs in on the sheet and opens no better than any stab binding.

The reason I have used this stapled binding in the past is that it is easy and quick to bind stacks of sheets for a presentable handout.

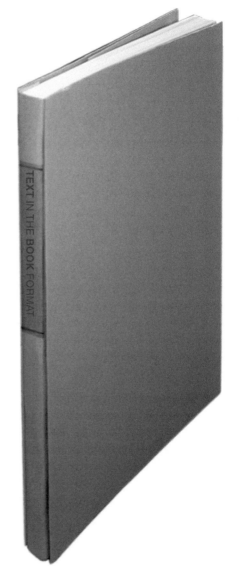

Z-fold cover on a stapled binding hides the staples on the outside and inside of the cover. The *Z*-fold on the facing page is shown prior to gluing.

276

The only thing I have added to the idea of staples used to make a binding is a *Z*-fold paper cover that hides the staples both on the outside of the cover as well as inside.

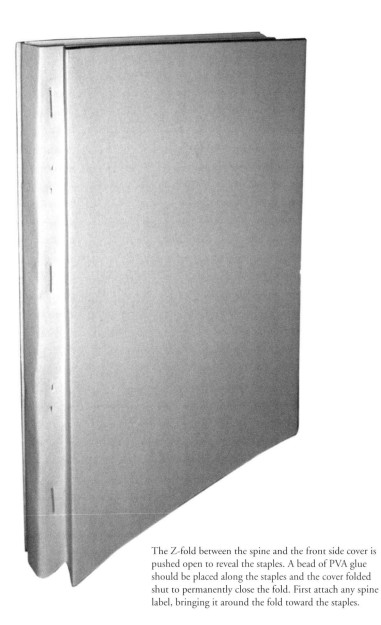

The Z-fold between the spine and the front side cover is pushed open to reveal the staples. A bead of PVA glue should be placed along the staples and the cover folded shut to permanently close the fold. First attach any spine label, bringing it around the fold toward the staples.

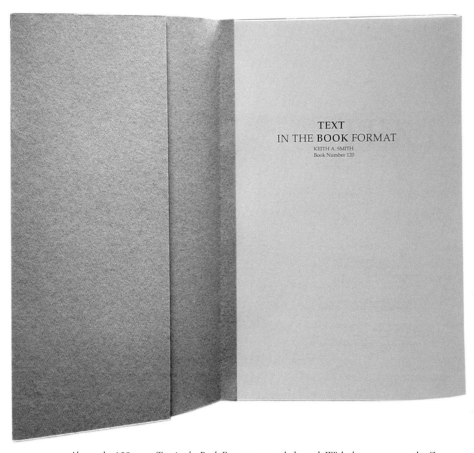

Above, the 128-page *Text in the Book Format* was staple-bound. With the cover open, the *Z*-fold extends 1/2″ in on the page at the spine edge, hiding the staples.

For a 1/2″ *Z*-fold, width of the cover must add 1″ for each *Z*-fold, one on each side of the spine, for a total of 2″. If there is a foredge turn-in, that width must be added, as well.

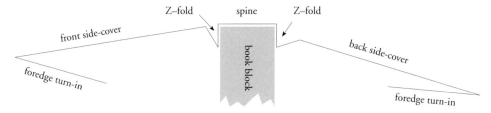

Cross-section showing how to fold the Z-Fold paper cover. It is critical to measure the book block compressed so the spine paper does not buckle.

Z-Folds at the Edges of the Spine

The *Z*-fold cover has 1/2″ folds along the spine edge of the cover that can be glued shut. Since the cover is made out of stiff paper which might be difficult to run through an inkjet printer, a spine-label can be printed on thin paper. The width of the label is wider than the spine. The vertical edges can be hidden inside the folds prior to gluing the *Z*-folds shut, as seen on page 277.

Several staplers will accept 1/4″, 3/8″ and 1/2″ staples. This one has a 2″ adjustable throat which allows the staples to be positioned in from the spine edge .
This stapler is a Bostitch™ B300HDS which uses SB35 staples. It can be purchased at a good hardware store, Office Max, Staples, et cetera. The handle provides good leverage so it is easy to staple through a hundred or more pages.

REFERENCES

GLOSSARY

Each term is defined with its first usage in the text of this manual. In the *Index of Terms,* page numbers are listed for important uses of key terms. The definitions below are used in this manual, as well as in other books on binding by Keith Smith.

3M Positionable Mounting Adhesive™ pressure-sensitive attachment bubbles on a roll of backing paper. The adhesive is transferred by pressure from the liner to paper or leather which is then adhered to book board with a squeegee.

accordion pleat 1. Several parallel, alternating and closely placed folds. Pleats are usually not pages, but an additional hinging device between the backbone and the attached folios or sections. Very often the pleat is the backbone, with separate side-covers rather than a flat back. Pleats also expand the depth of the backbone to accommodate additions to the book block. 2. Also known as the *concertina fold.*

across (also referred to as all across) 1. Perpendicular to the folds, cover to cover.[†] 2. Sewing which proceeds from section to section, generally in two or more separate sewings, using paired stations. Examples are *Blanket Stitch with Slit Strap, 2–Needle Coptic Sewing* and the *Celtic Weave.* Sewing across the spine is always more secure than sewing along the spine. If a thread breaks, only the sewing at those paired stations is affected. If the thread breaks sewing along the spine, the entire binding is compromised.

adhesive Generic for glue and paste. Glues used for binding remain pliable and are used on the backs over the sewing of most bindings. Glue on the backbone may be a heat glue, made from animals. It is archival in that it may be easily removed, but not in the sense it attracts insects which eat it. Another pliable glue is a poly-vinyl-acetate. Plastic based, PVA does not attract animals, but is not archival, inasmuch as it is not removable and thwarts attempts at book restoration. Pastes are used to adhere leather to spines, paper to paper and paper to boards. Wheat or rice paste are commonly used. See: *wheat paste.*

adhesive binding single leaf binding without sewing using a synthetic adhesive consolidation on the back.[*] Referred to as *perfect binding.*

against the grain Folding paper at right angles to the grain.

along (also referred to as *all along*) Parallel to the folds, head to tail.[†]

angle To move diagonally.[†]

[†] *GLOSSARY of TERMS, based on the work of Pamela Spitzmueller and Gary Frost,* a handout in a workshop by Betsy Palmer Eldridge.

[*] *A VOCABULARY of TERMS for BOOK CONSERVATION PRACTICE,* by Gary Frost

Asa-No-Ha Toji Japanese name for the stab binding also known as the *Hemp-Leaf Binding*. There are four traditional Japanese stab bindings. The others are the *Yotsume Toji,* or *Japanese 4—Hole Binding;* the *Kikko Toji,* or *Tortoise-Shell;* and the *Koki Toji,* or *Noble.* The Noble Binding is also referred to as the *Kangxi Binding,* after its reputed originator. These stab sewing are described in *Books without Paste or Glue,* Volume I of *Non-Adhesive Binding.*

back or backbone 1.The binding edge of a text prior to sewing or adhesive consolidation.˙

NOTE: The back differs from the spine, which is part of the cover which overlays this.

back saw Moulding saw or tenon saw used to cut the sewing stations when the book block is held in a finishing press.

backward (reverse) Counter to the direction of the sewing.†

bead 1. Top edge of the book (when viewing the book upright). 2. The little roll formed by the knot of an endband. See: *spine-bead* and *inside bead.*

beeswax Cake of wax usually purchased in a small block from a binder's supply. It is used for waxing all unwaxed thread, prior to sewing.

blind A type of book. See: *Venetian blind.*

blind embossing Stamping type into leather, without gold or foil.

board or **book board** A layered stock specifically for side-covers.

bodkin A sewing tool which is a type of awl. Unlike an awl which has a shaft which graduates in thickness, a bodkin has a thin metal shaft which remains constant in diameter except for narrowing at the point. It is similar to a *bradawl,* which is a carpenter's tool. An awl is inferior for piercing sewing stations, as it is difficult to obtain proper size of the opening in the paper. Choose a bradawl or bodkin which will make a hole slightly less than the diameter of the needle which will be used in the sewing.

bone or **bone folder** A flat, polished tool, made of bone, plastic or now, even Teflon™. Paper is folded by hand to a temporary fold. The bone is used to score the fold to a permanent position and to flatten the fold. This is done in a single stroke, as burnishing the paper will scar or make it shiny. A substitute is a dull stainless steel table knife which will not mar the paper.

book block or **text block** Total of the collated sections (signatures), folios, or sheets, constituting the body of a book.

book block pleat See: *concertina guard.*

booklet 1. A one-section binding. 2. A pamphlet. 3. A magazine.

bostrophedon A Germanic term meaning *as the ox plows.* In a single word, it graphically describes moving across a field, back and forth in a continuing *S* fashion. It is as if a page of text were read, the first line from left to right, the second from right to left and continued in this alternating manner. This movement and thus his term, describes the Scott McCarney binding. He also calls this the *snake format.*

bradawl A straight shafted awl with chisel edge used to make holes for brads or screws. Like the bodkin, a bradawl is ideal for piercing sewing stations in paper in bookbinding. Either tool is superior to an awl for piercing sewing stations.

butterfly sewing An across the spine sewing which utilizes paired stations. Each needle spans, enters the next section, then crosses inside to exit the other station. The Butterfly is also known as the *Yamato Toji,* or *Japanese 4–Needle Sewing.* It is a 12th century binding. The Butterfly is described in *Exposed Spine Sewings,* Volume III of *Non-Adhesive Binding.*

The Butterfly, or *Japanese 4–Needle Sewing,* is not to be confused with the Japanese 4–Hole Stab Binding, which is described in *Books without Paste or Glue,* Volume I of *Non-Adhesive Binding.*

case The two side-covers connected by spine-cloth or leather in a cased-in binding as opposed to a *cover* of two side-covers connected by spine-cloth or leather for a continuous support sewing.

catch-word In early printed books, the last word on a page was positioned at the foot. The same word was repeated at the top of the next page. Perhaps this served as a bridge in reading from page to page, but its purpose was a guide in collating signatures.

chain stitch "Chain stitch" is an embroidery term; it is not a stitch in bookbinding. In binding, the chain is a result of a succession of link stitches. *Link* is a stitch; *chain* is the resulting pattern.

to change over To continue sewing in a different section.[†]

clamshell A box for storing a book with a lid, hinged to open like covers.

climb To move upward.[†]

codex (plural: codices) A book, bound along one edge. One of the four types of books, the others being the fan, blind and the fold book.
NOTE: Many binders do not agree with this definition.

compiled section A section or signature constructed by assembling two or more folios, rather than folding down a sheet.

compound binding A hybrid book structure of two of the same or differing types of books. There are 4 types of books: the fan, the blind, oriental fold book and the western codex. Creating a structure of two or more of these types of books is a compound binding. Examples: 1. Sewing sections onto an accordion pleat for a concertina binding. 2. Including a fold book as a unit, along with sewing sections into a single spine.

concertina 1. A type of binding, utilizing the concertina fold. 2. The concertina fold is also called an accordion pleat.

concertina guard A form of construction securing sections to folded stubs with a pamphlet sewing and, in turn, sewing the stubs together to form a text block.[˙]

content Statement within the book of text and/or pictures. In a no-picture book, it is the cast shadows, cut shapes, holes, et cetera.

continuous support sewing Use of a single support, as opposed to sewing onto cords or tapes. The paperback sewings in *1– 2– & 3– Section Sewings,* Volume II of *Non-Adhesive Binding,* are examples, as are all but one sewing in *Quick Leather Bindings,* Volume V of *Non-Adhesive Binding.* It is important to reinforce the spine on paper covers by folding or pasting a second ply of paper in this area. Quarter leather cased-in or continuous support sewings can be reinforced with a strip of paper or Tyvek glued or adhered with PMA in the spine-gap.

to continue on To continue sewing in the same section.[†]

core A support. It might be a cord, or rolled material to form a cylindrical support, generally out of leather. The endband is formed on a core.

cover The two side-covers connected by the spine-cloth or leather for a continuous support sewing as opposed to a *case* of two side-covers connected by spine-cloth or leather in a cased-in binding.

cover stock or **cover weight** Heavy paper used for covers as opposed to text weight used for book blocks. Commercial printing papers generally come in both cover weight and text weight.

covering Forwarding is followed by Covering and Finishing. If the outside of the boards are not full leather or cloth, the area of the board that is not covered with cloth or leather is covered with decorative paper. The paste-down is made on the inside of the boards.

crease A fold induced by pressure marking or die debossing, not cutting. ˙ Some binders refer to this procedure as a score.

creep The successive protrusion from the outermost folio to the innermost within a section or signature.

crossbar The wooden dowel held above and parallel to the base of the sewing frame by threaded posts. The crossbar is often slotted to accept threaded hooks.

curl The distortion of a sheet due to differences in structure, coatings, or moisture from one side to the other.

deckle In papermaking, the width of the wet sheet as it comes off the wire of a paper machine.

deckled-edge The untrimmed feathery edges of paper formed where the pulp flows against the deckle.

digital scan Half-tone photographic images created on a computer scanner. I do not use the term *photograph,* reserving that dear term for silver prints.

display Presentation of the object, generally through turning pages. Books with one-sided display, the fan, blind and fold book might be displayed fully extended on a table, or wall displayed. Books with unusual formatting may be presented in the round as sculpture, the pages not meant to be turned.

dos-á-dos A specific traditional format of two connected codices which have a back cover in common.

drop To move downward.[†]

duodecimo aka **12to** 1. A sheet folded down to yield a section of 12 leaves or 24 pages. 2. Four folios, each slipped inside the other, to form a unit of sewing. See: *folio, quarto, sexto, octavo, sextodecimo* and *Z-fold*. In folding down a sheet to form a duodecimo, the first fold is against the grain, so that the final fold is with the grain.

endband Wrapping and beading decorative thread, usually of colored silk or cotton, at the head and tail of codices. Thread is wrapped around a core and periodically stitched into the book block. "Imitation" machine-made headbands are sold by the yard and pasted onto the backbone of commercial hard cover books.
NOTE: The term *headband* is often erroneously used, if the band described includes, or is specifically at the tail. Therefore, I use the term *endband,* rather than *headband,* as it includes the bands sewn at both the head and tail.

end cord A Cylinder of rolled cloth or leather, or a length of 4- or 6-ply cord. One length is placed at the head in the spine-gap between the side covers. The other at the tail prior to turning-in the cloth or leather. This gives some thickness to the material at the head and tail and gives a better look to the cover.

end paper In traditional binding, the sheet which is glued down on the inside of the cover board, extending across the gutter as the first page.

endsheets The first (and last) folio or section of a book may be blank and perhaps a nice laid paper in a particular color different from the bulk of the book block. Endsheets function as a mat surrounding a drawing. It is blank space to clear the mind before the introduction of the content of the opus.

enter To pass from the spine side to the fold side.[†]

exit To pass from the fold side to the spine side.[†]

F&G's (Folded and Gathered) The F&G's are the assembled signatures ready for sewing.

false kettle The (true) kettle stitch is the proper sewing procedure for ending one section, changing direction of movement in adding the next. The (true) kettle drops and links, slips and climbs. A false kettle would fail in one of these steps, usually failing to slip under in order to lock. True and false kettle stitches and link stitches in general are described in *Exposed Spine Sewings,* Volume III of *Non-Adhesive Binding* and in *Bookbinding for Book Artists.*

fan A book, bound at one point. One of the four types of books, the others being the blind, codex and the fold book. Fans and blinds are used by South Sea Island cultures.

finishing Finishing is decoration of the book after forwarding and covering.

first section In the sewing procedures, the term first does not necessarily mean the beginning of the book. On the bench, you may very well start sewing from the back, towards the front of the book. In that instance, the "first" section to be sewn is the final section of the book. See: *Face Up* and *Face Down,* in *Bookbinding for Book Artists.*

flat back Sewing without rounding the spine.

flat back cover Paper cover with two folds which delineate the spine from the side covers. These folds create the hinging action of the cover and are called *hinge-folds*.

flush cover 1. A cover whose front and back panels are the same dimensions as the pages. 2. In commercial binding, a cover that has been trimmed with the text block, so that cover and text block are the same size. See: *overhang cover*.

fold See: *accordion, hinge-fold, fold-out, gate fold* and *throw-out*.

fold book A book, whose binding is mechanical; the sheet is folded back and forth upon itself to create pages. One of the four types of books, the others being the fan, blind and the codex.

fold-out See: *throw-out*.

folio aka **fo** A folio is a sheet folded in half to yield four pages and two leaves. The fold is with the grain. The resulting folio will have the grain parallel with the spine. Folios can be units in binding, sewing through the fold-as-hinge. A folio can be slipped inside another folio to construct a quarto, rather than folding down a sheet to form a quarto. See: *quarto, sexto, octavo, duodecimo* and *Z-fold*.

foredge 1. The front edge of a book. (pronounced forrej). 2. The edge of the side cover and book block opposite the spine.

format The size, style, type page, margins, page set-up, et cetera.

forward In the direction on the sewing.†

forwarding After the book is sewn, forwarding is gluing the back, plowing, rounding and backing, sewing the endbands and attaching the boards. Forwarding is followed by covering and finishing.

gate fold Two facing fold-outs in a codex. Each fold-out is hinged on the foredges of an opened folio. When the gate fold is opened, or thrown-out, there are four facing pages, the two at each extreme extend beyond the book block.

gathering Assembling the folded signatures into the proper order for binding. See: *F&G's*.

grain The direction in which most fibers lie which corresponds with the direction the paper is made in commercial production machinery.

gutter 1. The blank space or inner margin, from printing area to binding.

half hitch A type of knot for tying-off, when there is only one loose end of thread: The needle slips under a stitch and is pulled until there is a small loop. The needle proceeds through the loop, before the thread is pulled tight. Half hitch is diagrammed in *Books without Paste or Glue*, Volume I of *Non-Adhesive Binding*, *Smith's Sewing Single Sheets*, Volume IV of *Non-Adhesive Binding* and *Bookbinding for Book Artists*.

head and **tail** The top and bottom of a book when stood upright. They are at right angles to the backbone or spine-edge and foredge.

headband and **tailband** Wrapping and beading decorative thread, usually of colored silk or cotton, at the head and tail of codices. Thread is wrapped around a core and periodically stitched into the book block. Imitation machine-made headbands are sold by the yard and pasted onto the backbone of commercial hard cover books.

NOTE: The term *headband* is often erroneously used, if the band described includes, or is specifically at the tail. Therefore, I use the term *endband,* rather than headband, as it includes the bands sewn at both the head and tail.

Hemp-Leaf Binding The stab binding also known as Asa-No-Ha Toji. There are four traditional Japanese stab bindings. The others are the Yotsume Toji, or Japanese 4—Hole Binding; the Kikko Toji, or Tortoise-Shell; and the Koki Toji, or Noble Binding, which is also referred to as the *Kangxi Binding,* after its reputed originator. Stab sewings are described in *Books without Paste or Glue,* Volume I of *Non-Adhesive Binding.*

hinge-fold The folds on either side of the spine, delineating the side covers from the spine-cover. See: *flat back cover.*

horizontal wrapper See: *wrapper.*

implied compound binding A inventive folding of pages or itinerary through a book that suggests a hybrid book structure of two of the same or differing types of books.

imposition The laying out of pages on a sheet, so that they will be in numerical order after the sheet is folded down as a folio or section or signature.

inner Between paired sewing stations. The approach to a station which is towards the center of the spine, rather than to the outer, which is near the spine-hinge. Inner should not be confused with the term *inside.*

inside The position on the valley side of a section, as opposed to the mountain peak, which is called the *outside.*

to the inside Toward the head or tail.[†]

inside bead In sewing Endbands as Change-Over, the sewing procedure results in beads on both sides of the packing. The bead on the spine side is referred to as the *spine-bead.* The bead facing the foredge is called the *inside bead.* See: *Two-Sided Beading* in *Exposed Spine Sewings,* Volume III of *Non-Adhesive Binding.*
I suggest you look at *Headbands, How To Work Them,* by Jane Greenfield & Jenny Hille.

jaconette A thin coated fabric used to reinforce a spine or joint in a book box.

Japanese 4–Needle Sewing The Japanese name for this sewing is Yamato Toji. It is a 12th century binding, also referred to as the *Butterfly Sewing.* Sewing is across the spine, utilizing paired stations. Each needle spans, enters the next section, then cross inside to exit the other station. The Japanese 4–Needle Sewing is not to be confused with the stab binding called the *Japanese 4–Hole Binding.* The Japanese 4–Needle Sewing sewing is described in *Exposed Spine Sewings,* Volume III of *Non-Adhesive Binding.*

Japanese 4—Hole Binding Japanese stab binding also known as the Yotsume Toji. There are four traditional Japanese stab bindings. The others are the Asa-No-Ha Toji, or Hemp-Leaf Binding; the Kikko Toji, or Tortoise-Shell; and the Koki Toji, or Noble Binding, which is also referred to as the *Kangxi Binding,* after its reputed originator. Stab sewings are described in *Books without Paste or Glue,* Volume I of *Non-Adhesive Binding.* The Japanese 4–Hole Stab Binding is not to be confused with the sewing across the spine, called the *Japanese 4–Needle Sewing.*

jog To knock down and to level an edge, preferably the head to keep text in registration.

Kangxi Binding Japanese name for the stab binding, named after its reputed originator. It is also known as the Noble, or the Koki Toji. There are four traditional Japanese stab bindings. The others are the Yotsume Toji, or Japanese 4—Hole Binding; the Kikko Toji, or Tortoise-Shell; the Asa-No-Ha Toji, or Hemp-Leaf Binding.
Stab sewings are described in *Books without Paste or Glue,* Volume I of *Non-Adhesive Binding.*

kerf or **kerf stations** Cuts made with a back saw across the section folds of an unsewn text. See: *sewing stations.*

kettle or **kettle stitch** Sewing procedure of ending one section, changing direction of movement in adding the next. The sewing drops backwards and links, slips and climbs. True and false kettle stitches and link stitches in general are described in Exposed Spine Sewings, Volume III of *Non-Adhesive Binding.*

key a 2–pronged metal unit, about the size of a key. A key for each cord rests under the slot in the base of a sewing frame temporarily tying the cord while the sewing proceeds.

Kikko Toji Japanese name for the stab binding known as the Tortoise-Shell Binding. There are four traditional Japanese stab bindings. The others are the Yotsume Toji, or Japanese 4—Hole Binding; the Asa-No-Ha Toji, or Hemp-Leaf Binding and the Koki Toji, or the Noble, or the Kangxi Binding, after its reputed originator. Stab sewings are described in *Books without Paste or Glue,* Volume I of *Non-Adhesive Binding.*

Koki Toji Japanese name for the stab binding known as the Noble, or the Kangxi Binding, after its reputed originator. There are four traditional Japanese stab bindings. The others are the Yotsume Toji, or Japanese 4—Hole Binding; the Kikko Toji, or Tortoise-Shell; the Asa-No-Ha Toji, or Hemp-Leaf Binding. Stab sewings are described in *Books without Paste or Glue,* Volume I of *Non-Adhesive Binding.*

lap To pass over a support or sewing thread.[†]

leaf 1. A sheet. 2. Two pages, back to back; a recto/verso.

link To pass under another thread.[†]

loop To circle around a support or sewing thread.[†]

moulding saw Backsaw or tenon saw used to cut the sewing stations when the book block is held in a finishing press.

Noble Binding Name of the Japanese stab binding known as the Koki Toji, or the Kangxi Binding, after its reputed originator. There are four traditional Japanese stab bindings. The others are the Yotsume Toji, or Japanese 4—Hole Binding; the Kikko Toji, or Tortoise-Shell; and the Asa-No-Ha Toji, or Hemp-Leaf Binding. Stab sewings are described in *Books without Paste or Glue,* Volume I of *Non-Adhesive Binding.*

octavo aka **8vo** 1. A sheet folded in half three times, to yield a section of 16 pages with 8 leaves. 2. Three folios, each slipped inside the other, to form a unit of sewing. A sextodecimo, or 16mo, has 32 pages with 16 leaves. See: *folio, quarto, sexto, octavo, duodecimo, sextodecimo* and *Z-fold*. In folding down a sheet to form an octavo, the first fold is with the grain; the second is against and the third is with the grain. The resulting section will have the grain parallel with the spine.

one-of-a-kind A book conceived and executed as a single copy. The word *unique,* meaning "special" should not be used to define a single copy item, as the term *unique* applies to production work as well.
NOTE: Some librarians define a book as an item which must have more than one copy by definition. Consequently, they do not recognize or purchase one-of-a-kinds. On one occasion I was dismayed at this reasoning of a librarian who could not consider purchasing a one-of-a-kind. The librarian said it was the wrong department and said take it to the museum on campus to the sculpture curator! — What would happen if this librarian should happen to run across an ancient book, of which only that single copy survived? Would they say it no longer a "book", but now, sculpture?

1–on Sewing 1–on applies to sewing multi-section (multi-signature) sewings along the spine: In addition to using the kettle stations at the head and tail, every sewing station is used. The middle stations lap or loop the supports.

open ended Open ended stations refer to the use of the head and the tail as sewing stations. The support is not pierced. It is a passive station, that is, the thread wraps around the head or tail, marking the change-over.

opened folio The two facing pages at any point to which the codex is opened.

Oriental fold book See: *fold book.*

outer Towards the outside of paired sewing stations, rather than centrally, between. Outer should not be confused with the term *outside*.

outside The position on the mountain peak of a section, as opposed to the valley, which is called the *inside.*

to the outside Away from the head or tail.[†]

overhand knot aka **overhand *k*** Half a square knot. For instructions how to tie, see: *Knots* in either *Books without Paste or Glue,* Volume I of *Non-Adhesive Binding*; *Bookbinding for Book Artists* or *Smith's Sewing Single Sheets,* Volume IV of *Non-Adhesive Binding.*

overhang cover A cover larger in size than the pages it encloses. The amount of the side cover that extends beyond the book block, bordering the head, foredge and tail is called the *square*. See: *flush cover.*

pack To loop several times around.[†]

page 1. One side of an unfolded sheet. 2.That portion of a folio or section or signature bordered by folds and/or the edge of the sheet.

paired stations Sewing directly across the spine employs two sewing stations. Other paired stations along the spine are sewn independently. Each paired station uses one thread and two needles.

pamphlet 1. A one-section text. 2. A booklet. 3. Type of sewing for a booklet.

pamphlet sewing Type of sewing used to bind a booklet. The pamphlet sewing uses a *"B"* stitch, as opposed to a figure *8* stitch. Pamphlet sewing is described in *Books without Paste or Glue, 1– 2– & 3–Section Sewings, Bookbinding for Book Artists,* as well as in this manual.

The term *pamphlet stitch* should be avoided, as it is a sewing, not a stitching. *Pamphlet stitch sewing* is correct, but awkward.

paste See: *adhesive* and *wheat paste.*

perfect bound 1. Adhesive binding without sewing or stitching. 2. Binding of a book which has no sewing and no folds on the backbone. The book therefore has no sections, signatures or folios, only a stack of sheets. The back is glued. Commercial paperbacks are generally (imperfectly) perfect bound. Thus, unfortunately there is a general low esteem for any book with paper covers. In the past, the main difference between trade books which were paperback and hard cover, was the latter was sewn. Now, many publishers are reducing the quality of their hard covers and are using perfect binding, rather than sewing them.

pleat An Oriental fold used to attach sections, rather than as a complete book in itself. Attachment is usually with a pamphlet sewing. Pleat is also known as a concertina, concertina guard, or accordion fold. See: *accordion pleat.*

ply In this text, the term is used as one piece of paper, rather than the process of making paper in layers. Two-ply is only used in this text to mean a sheet folded back upon itself for reinforcement, or two surfaces glued together. The term is never used to mean *duplex,* a type of commercially made paper with a different color on each side of the sheet.

PMA See: *3M Positionable Mounting Adhesive.*

production books Books made in an edition, whether by hand, or published.

pull factor The characteristic of leather, some papers and fabrics to stretch when wet and to shrink or pull when they dry. In pasting these items to boards, it is not using a press, but the counter-balancing of the pull factor which prevents board warpage. See: *Warpage,* in either *Bookbinding for Book Artists* or *Smith's Sewing Single Sheets,* Volume IV of *Non-Adhesive Binding.*

punch Metal cylindrical tool with sharpened hollow shaped end for cutting and solid head for striking with a hammer to cut through paper. Shapes are usually various diameters of circles and, rarely, squares, diamonds, oblongs.

quarto aka **4to** 1. A sheet folded in half twice, to yield a section of four leaves or eight pages. 2. Two folios, one slipped inside the other, to form a unit of sewing. See: *folio, sexto, octavo, duodecimo, sextodecimo* and *Z-fold*.

In folding down a sheet to form a quarto, the first fold is against the grain; the second is with the grain. The resulting section will have the grain parallel with the spine.

ream Five hundred sheets of paper.

recto/verso Two pages, back to back; a leaf. Recto is a right hand page. Verso is the back of that leaf, not the page facing the recto in the opened folio.

NOTE: Recto does not mean front; verso does not mean back. A recto or a verso is a front side when it is viewed. Each becomes a back when the page is turned and it is not in view. Recto/verso is convenient terminology for folding and collating signatures.

saddle wire or **saddle stitch** In commercial binding, to fasten a booklet by wiring it through the fold or the side of the single section. The machine is adjusted to the thickness of the opened section and uses a spool of wire. It is looped through the section, cut and crimped, similar to stapling.

score 1. To indent with a bone folder, but not cutting. 2. A light surface cut made to facilitate folding or flexing in card or board. See: *crease.*

section 1. A sheet folded down to yield eight or more pages, such as a quarto, sexto or duodecimo. 2. Two or more loose folios compiled to form a quarto, sexto or duodecimo, et cetera. A section can be blank paper, or printed. If printed, then it is specifically a *signature.*

NOTE: To avoid confusion of terms in this book, *section i*s never used to mean a portion, or a chapter of the book.

NOTE 2: If the sheet has been printed, then folded down, it is referred to in printers' terminology as a *signature.* Any signature can be called a *section,* but only a section which has been printed is technically a signature. See: *signature.*

self cover A cover of the same paper as the text block.

sew a set To sew one more than one section on at a time.[†]

sewing 1–on See: *1–on.*

sewing path The journey of the needle and thread, in and out of the sewing stations, in constructing a sewing.

sewing stations 1. The mark, or the pierce along the spine fold of the cover and the backbone of the section, or folio showing the positions of the sewing. The supports are the stations, rather than the holes. Each tape requires a hole on either side. The two holes per tape are not the sewing station, but merely the holes. The tape is the sewing station. 2. Path of the needle through paper to create the sewing on the spine. If made with a saw, they are called *kerf stations.* See: *sewn vs stitched.*

sewing 2–on See: *2–on.*

sewn vs stitched Sewing refers to the thread path along the valley and mountain peak, as opposed to set in from the fold. That is stabbing. Stabbing is stitching, not sewing. Path of the needle limited to the gutter is not "stitching", but sewing. Sewing is done with stitches. Therefore, "stitches" is appropriate when referring to sewing in the fold, but stitching equals stabbing.

sexto aka **6to** A sheet folded down to create a section of 6 leaves, or 12 pages. The sheet is first folded against the grain with a *Z*-fold, dividing the sheet into thirds. That is then folded in half with the grain. See: *folio, quarto, octavo, duodecimo, sextodecimo* and *Z-fold.*

sextodecimo aka **16mo** A sheet folded down to create a section of 32 pages with 16 leaves. See: *folio, quarto, sexto, octavo, duodecimo* and *Z-fold.*

sheet 1. An unfolded piece of paper. 2. A leaf. 3. The full size of the paper before being folded down into a folio or section. 4. In single sheet bindings, a sheet is two pages back to back; a recto/verso. A sheet is one piece of paper, consisting of two pages. It is not a section, since it has no fold as a hinge. Sheets can be folded down as folios or sections. Without being folded down, a sheet can still be a unit of sewing. However, a sheet is limited as a book element: The full sheet, without a fold, can only be used in a stab binding, a single sheet pamphlet sewing, or an album binding. All of these are described in *Books without Paste or Glue,* Volume I of *Non-Adhesive Binding.*

side cover Front and back cover, as opposed to the spine.

signature A specific type of section, differing from the general term of section, in that a signature is a sheet that first has been printed, then folded down. A signature is a section, but a section is not necessarily a signature. Signature is a printer's term; section is a binder's term.

simple/compound Terms used only to differentiate basic bindings from hybrids constructed by combining two or more basic types of books.

slip (v.) To pass under itself.[†]

slips (n.) The ends of tapes, cords, or supporting straps attached to the covers.

slit Slit is a severing with a knife. It has length, but no width. See: *slot.*

slot A slot is an opening, constructed by two slits, parallel and no more than about 1/8" apart. Slots, rather than slits, are needed to accommodate the thickness of the inserted photographs, or weaving a strap or flap, to help prevent buckling of the sheet.

Smythe-sewn Commercial method of machine-stitching a book. See: *sewn vs stitched* in the Glossary.

spacers A stub added to the mountain peak to be sewn with the folio. It expands the spine the same amount as the (photo) insert for that page. After the inserts are added, the foredge of the album will not bulge wider than the spine.

span To climb and change over to another section.[†]

spine or **spine-cover** 1. The depth of a bound book, connecting the two side covers. The spine-covers the back, or backbone. 2. That part of the book that is visible when it is on the shelf. It is sometimes referred to as the *backstrip*.

spine-bead In sewing Endbands as Change-Over, the sewing procedure results in beads on both sides of the packing. The bead on the spine side is referred to as the *spine-bead*. The bead facing the foredge is called the *inside bead*. See: *Two-Sided Beading* in *Exposed Spine Sewings,* Volume III of *Non-Adhesive Binding.*

spine paper A strip of paper or Tyvek adhered to the inside of the leather on the spine between the side covers to reinforce the sewing stations.

square or **square of the book** 1. The projection of the side cover beyond the book block. 2. Only the part of the cover that extends beyond the book block and borders the head, foredge and tail. The total surface of the cover is referred to as an *overhang cover.*

square knot or **Reef knot** For instructions how to tie, see: *Knots* in either *Books without Paste or Glue,* Volume I of *Non-Adhesive Binding; Bookbinding for Book Artists* or *Smith's Sewing Single Sheets,* Volume IV of *Non-Adhesive Binding.*

station or **sewing station** 1. A place where the sewing stops to attach a section to other sections or to a common support or to both.[†] 2. Passive sewing stations is the use of the head and tail as change-over. This is referred to as open ended. In diagramming sewings with endbands as change-cover, I assign the support, usually cords, at the head and the tail a sewing station number. They are not pierced sewing stations, but passive, that is, open ended. This makes for easy reference in the drawn illustrations. See: *paired stations.*

stitching See: *sewn vs stitched* in the Glossary.

strap Horizontal supports across the spine onto which supported sewings are made. The strap is usually separate from the cover and attached after the sewing. In the Buttonhole Binding, the straps are sections of the spine.

stub Cutting out a page/s from a Tight Back, close to the spine edge, after it is bound to make space for an insert which will not bulge the spine. For a Flat Back, spacers are used.

suminagashi "The original and easiest method of marbling, inks flowing freely on water, producing meandering lines of color." –Diane Vogel Maurer with Paul Maurer, *Marbling, A Complete Guide to Creating Beautiful Patterned Papers and Fabrics.*

super Super is a kind of stiffened gauze, sometimes referred to as *tarlatan, crash,* or *mull.*

supported sewings Sections sewn together around common straps, tapes or cords, which go across the back, perpendicular to it. The supports are generally attached to side covers.

swell Thickness added to the backbone by the accumulation of sewing threads or any guards. See: *Choosing the Thread* in *Bookbinding for Book Artists.* Also, see: *Swelling the Backbone* in *Books without Paste or Glue,* Volume I of *Non-Adhesive Binding* and expanding the spine pleat also in *Books without Paste or Glue. Swell* is also discussed to a lesser degree in *Smith's Sewing Single Sheets,* Volume IV of *Non-Adhesive Binding.*

tab A narrow strip woven as means of attachment.

tail 1. The bottom edge of a book when standing upright. 2. The edge opposite the head and perpendicular to the spine and foredge.

tailband See: *headband* and *endband.*

NOTE: The term *headband* is often erroneously used, if the band described includes, or is specifically at the tail. Therefore, I use the term *endband,* rather than headband, as it includes the bands sewn at both the head and tail.

tapes Woven fabric supports, usually linen, onto which the sewing occurs. They are usually 1/4" wide and always are non-adhesive.

tenon saw Moulding saw or backsaw used to cut the sewing stations when the book block is held in a finishing press.

tension Regulation of tautness. Uniform shape and tautness is desired. Betsy Palmer Eldridge says that the tension varies with each sewer. It varies even if one person stops for a break. It is best to start and sew the entire book at once. The operative word is snug. Tension should not be loose, but neither should it be tight. I find that men tend to sew too tightly. Link stitches lose their teardrop shape when pulled tightly.

text block See: *book block.*

tie-off Joining two threads with a knot at the beginning or end of a sewing.

ties-down The threads which extend from the endband, in on the spine to the next station to anchor the endband. The tie-off may enter a station on the section, or link under a support at that station.

throw-out A fold-out. The action of unfolding of a fold-out or throw-out is referred to as *thrown-out.* A throw-out might be a single fold, gate fold, or any other page which is larger than the book block and folded down for storage. Traditionally refers to a fold-out at the end of a book containing a map. The map is thrown-out, so that it remains visible while any other page in the book can be read and turned. A throw-out has the fold at the foredge. A throw-down has the fold at the tail. A throw-up has the fold at the head.

Tortoise-Shell Binding The Japanese stab binding, also known as the Kikko Toji. There are four traditional Japanese stab bindings. The others are the Yotsume Toji, or Japanese 4—Hole Binding; the Asa-No-Ha Toji, or Hemp-Leaf Binding and the Koki Toji, or the Noble Binding. The Noble Binding is also referred to as the *Kangxi Binding,* after its reputed originator. Stab sewings are described in *Books without Paste or Glue,* Volume I of *Non-Adhesive Binding.*

2–on   Sewing 2–on applies to sewing multi-section (multi-signature) sewings along the spine: With the exception of the first two and final two, sections (signatures) the remaining sections (signatures) do not use all the sewing stations, except for the kettle stations at the head and tail. The sewing alternates back and forth between two sections being sewn on at once. Therefore, not all the middle stations are used.

types of books   There are four basic types of books, determined by how they are bound:

1.   at one point is called a *fan*.
2.   at two points is the Venetian blind. The fan and blind are used by South Sea Island cultures.
3.   across one edge, is the western codex.
4.   alternate folds back and forth upon itself is the Oriental fold book. The other three types of books are sewn. The fold book's binding is mechanical.

Tyvek™   An inert sheet of considerable strength and water-tight manufactured for insulating buildings by DuPont. Its strength and pH neutral appeal make it a good sheet to reinforce bindings. Available unprinted in sheets from paper companies.

unsupported sewings   Sections sewn directly together, without common straps, tapes or cords.

Venetian blind or **blind**   A book, bound at two points. One of the four types of books, the others being the fan, codex and the fold book. Fans and blinds are used by South Sea Island cultures.

verso   See: *recto/verso*.

vertical wrapper   See: *wrapper*.

wheat paste   An adhesive, like rice paste, used to adhere leather to the spine and decorative papers to the board. For formulas of making wheat paste, see: *Wheat Paste*, in *Bookbinding for Book Artists*, or in *Smith's Sewing Single Sheets*, Volume IV of *Non-Adhesive Binding*.

with the grain   Folding paper parallel to the grain of the paper.

wrapped stations   Head and tail of the sections used as sewing stations. Passive, as opposed to a pierced or slit stations. Open ended.

wrapper   Paper covering board covers without the use of adhesives. See: *Flat Back with Boards* and *Separately Wrapped Boards* in *Books without Paste or Glue*, Volume I of *Non-Adhesive Binding*.

Yamato Toji   Japanese name for the 4–needle sewing, across the spine. It is also referred to as the *Japanese 4–Needle Sewing*, as well as the *Butterfly Sewing*. It is sewn across the spine, utilizing paired stations. Each needle spans, enters the next section, then cross inside to exit the other station. Yamato Toji is described in *Exposed Spine Sewings*, Volume III of *Non-Adhesive Binding*.
Yamato Toji, or Japanese 4–Needle Sewing, is not to be confused with the the Japanese 4–Hole Stab Binding, which is described in *Books without Paste or Glue*, Volume I of *Non-Adhesive Binding*.

Yotsume Toji Japanese name for the stab binding also known as the Japanese 4—Hole Stab Binding. There are four traditional Japanese stab bindings. The others are the Asa-No-Ha Toji, or Hemp-Leaf Binding; the Kikko Toji, or Tortoise-Shell; and the Koki Toji, or Noble Binding, which is also referred to as the *Kangxi Binding,* after its reputed originator. Stab sewings are described in *Books without Paste or Glue,* Volume I of *Non-Adhesive Binding.*

Z-Fold Procedure to create a 12 and a 24 page section. The sheet is first folded in thirds, against the grain (the Z-fold). Folding the Z-fold in half once, with the grain, gives a sexto. Folding the sexto in half with the grain gives 12 leaves, or 24 pages. It is called a *duodecimo.* See: *folio, quarto, sexto, octavo, duodecimo* and *sextodecimo.*

INDEX OF TERMS

CENTIMETERS TO INCHES

1cm =	0.39"	35	13.78	69	27.17
2	0.79	36	14.17	70	27.56
3	1.18	37	14.57	71	27.95
4	1.57	38	14.96	72	28.35
5	1.97	39	15.35	73	28.74
6	2.36	40	15.75	74	29.13
7	2.76	41	16.14	75	29.53
8	3.15	42	16.54	76	29.92
9	3.54	43	16.93	77	30.31
10	3.94	44	17.32	78	30.71
11	4.33	45	17.72	79	31.10
12	4.72	46	18.11	80	31.50
13	5.12	47	18.50	81	31.89
14	5.51	48	18.90	82	32.28
15	5.91	49	19.29	83	32.68
16	6.30	50	19.69	84	33.07
17	6.69	51	20.08	85	33.46
18	7.09	52	20.47	86	33.86
19	7.48	53	20.87	87	34.25
20	7.87	54	21.26	88	34.65
21	8.27	55	21.65	89	35.04
22	8.66	56	22.05	90	35.43
23	9.06	57	22.44	91	35.83
24	9.45	58	22.83	92	36.22
25	9.84	59	23.23	93	36.61
26	10.24	60	23.62	94	37.01
27	10.63	61	24.02	95	37.40
28	11.02	62	24.41	96	37.80
29	11.42	63	24.80	97	38.19
30	11.81	64	25.20	98	38.58
31	12.20	65	25.59	99	38.98
32	12.60	66	25.98	100	39.37
33	12.99	67	26.38		
34	13.39	68	26.77		

INDEX OF ILLUSTRATIONS

INDEX OF NAMES

BOOKS *on* BOOKS

Concept

Structure of the Visual Book, keith smith *BOOKS,* Third Edition 1994, discusses concepts of ordering a book of pictures by means of a group, series, or sequence. Pacing is stressed by composing the pages as well as the individual pictures. Utilizing the space between pictures is part of the awareness of time in books. 240 pages with 198 photographic illustrations by 53 book artists.

paperback or in sheets: $25

ISBN 0–9637682–1–2

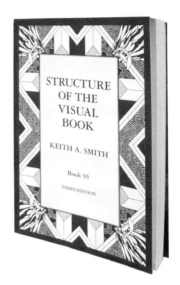

Concept

Text in the Book Format, keith smith *BOOKS,* Second Edition, 1995, is a concern for conceiving text as a book experience. This differs from writing a running manuscript or the single sheet format. A book experience cannot be fully revealed in a recitation but demands holding the physical object and turning pages conceived as part of the content. This approach does not treat the book format as a vessel, but allows writing to emanate from the inherent properties of the book—the opposite of sticking words into the object. 128 pages.

paperback or in sheets: $17.50

ISBN 0–9637682–3–9

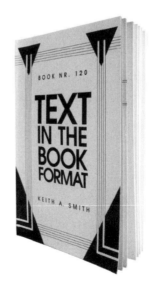

How To Bind

Non–Adhesive Binding, Volume I: *Books without Paste or Glue,* keith smith *BOOKS,* The Revised & Expanded Edition, 1999. Introduction covers binding, paper, sewing, knots and tools. This is followed by detailed written instructions for 32 simple to complex sewings. The procedures are also presented as 320 drawings, diagrammed step by step. 116 photographic reproductions of bindings by 37 contemporary binders and artists. 352 pages.

paperback or in sheets: $30
ISBN 0–9637682–6–3

How To Bind

Non–Adhesive Binding, Volume II: *1– 2– & 3–Section Sewings,* keith smith *BOOKS,* First Edition, 1995. Written and drawn illustrations for 122 sewings which yield four, to perhaps a hundred pages imposed as one, two or three sections. Almost all of these sewings on continuous limp paper supports were devised by Smith, as the book was written. Photos of bindings by 28 contemporary binders and artists. 320 pages.

paperback or in sheets: $30
ISBN 0–9637682–2–0

All the books are printed on archival paper. Available either as Smythe sewn paperback, or, *in sheets,* folded and gathered sections, if you wish to hand bind your own copy.
Individuals or stores can order directly from keith smith *BOOKS.*
Besides store discounts, there are group discounts available for individuals ordering 6 or more assorted titles. Email for information, or check the web site.

How To Bind

Non–Adhesive Binding, Volume III: *Exposed Spine Sewings,* keith smith *BOOKS,* First Edition, 1995. Variations on raised support sewings with packed cords or endbands as change–over rather than using kettle stitches. Descriptions of sewings across the spine include 2–Needle Coptic, Greek Binding, Celtic Weave and Caterpillar. Most of the sewings were devised by Smith as the book was written. Nine various Coptic sewings are described. Photographic illustrations by contemporary binders are shown. 320 pages.

paperback or in sheets: $30
ISBN 0–9637682–4–7

How to Bind

Non–Adhesive Binding, Volume IV: *Smith's Sewing Single Sheets,* keith smith *BOOKS,* First Edition, 2001. These sewings can be used to bind sections, and/or single sheets of paper, board, plexiglass and even metal. The bindings open flat to any page, unlike traditional post-bindings and stab bindings commonly used to bind single sheets. This attribute makes handsome and functional albums for photographs. Smith devised these sewings to make one-of-a-kind books from large inkjet prints. There are 5 Coptic sewings, 2 sewing raised cord and 1 sewing onto tapes—all with single sheets.

paperback or in sheets: $30
ISBN 0–9637682–8–X

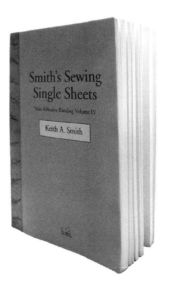

To order, or for a free brochure on all titles, contact:
keith smith *BOOKS,* 1115 East Main Street, Suite 219, Box 8
Rochester, New York 14609–6152 USA
Tel/Fax: 585 482 2496 or Email: keith@keithsmithbooks.com
Web Site: www.keithsmithbooks.com

How to Bind

Bookbinding for Book Artists, First Edition, 1998, keith smith *BOOKS.*

Bookbinding for Book Artists presents a simple approach to binding in cloth or leather. It eliminates the skill required to pare leather or to sew endbands. Household tools are substituted for traditional binding equipment.

Three bindings are described:

• Pamphlet Binding with Boards gives a substantial presentation of a book with only 4 to 32 pages. This hard cover book is presented as quarter cloth, half or full cloth. It is described both with the endsheets as paste–down, as well as exposed cloth hinges on the inside of the boards. This binding gives a substantial presentation for small projects.

• Flat Back is ideal for medium size projects. Shown as sewn onto tapes, it gives a book of 24 to 100 pages. It is the most commonly used binding for hard cover artists books.

• Tight Back and the Hollow Back variation are presented as leather bound books, rounded and backed. The arch structurally allows a book to be bound with hundreds of pages. Yet, this elegant binding can have as few as 32 pages.

Bookbinding for Book Artists has over 400 detailed drawn illustrations to augment the text. They are the most elaborate illustrations in Smith's books–on–books to date.

The book contains 60 photo reproductions of books by 19 contemporary binders and book artists. 432 pages.

paperback or in sheets: $35
ISBN 0–9637682–5–5

Autobiography

200 Books, An Annotated Bibliography, First Edition, July 2000, keith smith *BOOKS.*

200 Books is a memoir as told through all the books made by the author.

Text and pictures describe the 199 previous books by Smith with over 550 photo reproductions. The text gives background of the author and describes why each book was made with references to other artists. Sometimes there are detailed descriptions of how the imagery was technically achieved. 336 pages.

hard cover or in sheets: $35

ISBN: 0–9637682–7–1

www.keithsmithbooks.com

For each of the nine titles many color reproductions of bindings are shown as well as elaborately described on my web site. You can order books with a credit card or just browse through the pictures and descriptions.

ACKNOWLEDGMENTS

- My thanks to all my readers.
- Scott McCarney

    Once again I thank my partner, Scott, for his patience and understanding.
- Gail Ferris

    Gail chided me into designing a color cover. That was a good idea.

    Many thanks to Gail for proofreading and comments, and including her protest that my drawings are from the viewpoint of a left-handed person. Gail wrote in the margin on page 111, "You are catering to 5% of your readers. See chart." She had taped a statistics comparison table to that page which shows strongly left-sided people are 5% of the population.

    I told her when I have to pay extra for left-handed scissors and every time I have to hold a butter knife upside down it reinforces *my* books will be left-handed friendly. Sorry, Gail. No doubt when you proofread my next book you will include your rebuttal.

COLOPHON

Book Number 211
was written from October 2001–July 2002 on a Mac Double Processor
G4. Text was written in Quark XPress, formatted as it was written.
Bindings were devised and then some photographed with a Nikon
Coolpix 700™ digital camera. Later bindings were photographed with a
Nikon Coolpix 5000. After downloading a picture and removing the
background, the PhotoShop document of an isolated book was placed
onto the page *as* I was writing the accompanying text. Text and/or photo
were adjusted to the composition of the page.

Quick Leather Bindings
was periodically proofed on an Hewlett Packard LaserJet 4MV. The book
was sent to the printer on CD, postscript, for direct platemaking at 1270
dots per inch for the type, 200 dpi for the EPS files and 150 line screen
for the drawings made in FreeHand™.

Typeface is Adobe Garamond.

Photographs of the bindings are by the author, as well as the drawn and
photo–digital illustrations and the cover design.

This second printing of the First Edition is offset in 1000 copies on Finch
Vellum 80 lb. text and cover with film lamination. The book is Smythe
sewn, paperback. An additional 200 copies are available unbound, folded
and gathered, for anyone who might wish to hand bind their own copy of
this book.

Keith A. Smith
April 2011

KE TH

Woven and Interlocking Book Structures

3 June 2002. Today I received the photograph below from Claire, along with a copy of a fantastic new book that you must see:

Woven and Interlocking Book Structures by Claire Van Vliet and Elizabeth Steiner
from the Janus, Steiner and Gefn Presses. ISBN 0-9620640-4-1

Photograph by Claire Van Vliet taken at the Sydney, Australia airport.
Thanks, Claire, and my congratulations to you, my good friend Elizabeth and all involved.